THE WILD EAST

THE WILD EAST

Negotiating the Russian financial frontier

PETER WESTIN

Published by **Pearson Education**

London · New York · San Francisco · Toronto · Sydney
Tokyo · Singapore · Hong Kong · Cape Town · Madrid
Paris · Milan · Munich · Amsterdam

PEARSON EDUCATION LIMITED

Head Office:
Edinburgh Gate
Harlow CM20 2JE
Tel: +44 (0)1279 623623
Fax: +44 (0)1279 431059

London Office:
128 Long Acre
London WC2E 9AN
Tel: +44 (0)20 7447 2000
Fax: +44 (0)20 7240 5771
Website: www.financialminds.com

_____

First published in Great Britain in 2001

The right of Peter Westin to be identified as Author
of this Work has been asserted by him in accordance
with the Copyright, Designs and Patents Act 1988.

ISBN 1 903 68409 9

British Library Cataloguing-in-Publication Data
A catalogue record for this book is available from the British Library.

10 9 8 7 6 5 4 3 2 1

Typeset by Pantek Arts Ltd, Maidstone, Kent.
Printed and bound in Great Britain by Biddles Ltd., Guildford and Kings Lynn

The publisher's policy is to use paper manufactured from sustainable forests.

CONTENTS

ACKNOWLEDGEMENTS

The idea to produce this book first came to me during my time in Moscow as editor of *Russian Economic Trends.* Despite the piles, stacked atop my collage of a desktop, of books, journals and articles devoted to the ills and shortcomings of Russia's transition economy and featuring innumerable tales of investors' woes, I discovered that no single volume brought together the voices of the frontline. I mean the market makers: the ones who have spent hours stuck in bureaucracy, fighting for their rights as shareholders, reaping huge gains and suffering staggering losses. But also, the ones who pulled through the crisis of August 1998 and felt the winds of change.

I am most grateful to the contributors for taking their time away from (often, but not always) much more profitable activities, and sharing their perspectives and experience, in effect making this publication possible.

A special tribute goes to Professor Erik Berglöf who, during my sojourn at the Stockholm Institute of Transition Economics (SITE), allowed me the time to develop this book. I am also grateful to Jody Lanfrey at SITE for her advice on the structure and concept of the book. Ben Hooson contributed his excellent editing skills to the project. Furthermore, I would like to thank my friends and colleagues at SITE and the Centre for Economic and Financial Research (CEFIR) in Moscow for providing an outstanding intellectual environment.

Peter Westin

THE AUTHORS

Kasper Bartholdy. *Chief economist for emerging markets in Europe, the Middle East and Africa at Credit Suisse First Boston.* Kasper Bartholdy started his career as a management consultant in 1984 after graduating from the Universities of Copenhagen and Aarhus with degrees in Economics, Computer Science and Journalism. After a five-year spell as an economist with the IMF in Washington, D.C. (1986–91), he was a lead economist at the EBRD (1991–6). He joined CSFB in January 1997 and became a managing director in January 2001.

Erik Berglöf. *Director of the Stockholm Institute of Transition Economics (SITE) at the Stockholm School of Economics.* Erik Berglöf is a research fellow of CEPR and the William Davidson Institute at the University of Michigan. He was previously assistant professor at ECARE, Université Libre de Bruxelles, and has held visiting positions at Stanford University.

He has written extensively on financial contracting and corporate governance. In particular, he has applied theoretical insights to the study of differences between financial systems, and specific ownership and control arrangements. More recently, his work has focused on bankruptcy. He has also been involved in several capacity-building initiatives in transition countries, including as director of the Center for Economics and Financial Research (CEFIR) in Moscow and the Baltic International Center for Economic Policy Studies (BICEPS) in Riga.

Mr Berglöf has served as special advisor to the prime minister of Sweden, the Russian government, and on several government commissions and EU-related panels. In addition, he is a consultant to the World Bank and the IMF.

Stephan Boven. *Principal banker at the Group for Small Business, European Bank of Reconstruction and Development.* After completing his university studies, Stephan Boven became a staff member of a Frankfurt-based consultant company concentrating on micro and small enterprise (MSE) lending. From 1995 to 1997 he worked as a bank advisor in Siberia and Moscow in the framework of the Russia Small Business Fund, in both the micro loan component and the small loan component, followed by a series of short-term missions in Eastern Europe targeted at the preparation and implementation of MSE lending projects.

In 1999, Mr Boven joined the European Bank for Reconstruction and Development where he is mainly responsible for projects targeting the establishment of commercial micro-finance banks.

Al Breach. *Russia economist, Goldman Sachs.* Al Breach studied maths and philosophy as an undergraduate at the University of Edinburgh, after which he completed a Masters in Economics at the London School of Economics and worked briefly in the City of London before travelling to Moscow via Beijing in the summer of 1996 to write *Russian Economic Trends* at the Russian European Centre for Economic Policy (RECEP). In late September 1998 he joined Goldman Sachs, first as a consultant and then as staff, working as the company's Russia (and other CIS and East European countries) economist based in Moscow.

Roman Filatov. *Vice president, investment analyst, Templeton Asset Management Ltd.* Roman Filatov joined the Templeton organization in 1996. As an investment analyst he is responsible for equity research of Russian companies. Prior to joining Templeton, Mr Filatov worked at Deloitte & Touche CIS, where he audited several large Russian institutions, and before that was an analyst at Mezhcombank (Moscow). Mr Filatov holds a Master of Science degree from the Moscow Institute of Physics and Technology and is a Level II Chartered Financial Analyst (CFA) candidate.

Yevgeny Gavrilenkov. *Deputy head of the Bureau for Economic Analysis.* Yevgeny Gavrilenkov is one of Russia's leading macroeconomists. In this capacity, he has advised several Russian heads of government. He has played, and continues to play, a key role in the drafting and further development of the Russian government's macroeconomic programme, and was responsible for the macroeconomic part of the economic strategy adopted by the new government.

Professor Gavrilenkov is also Professor in Applied Macro economics at the Higher School of Economics in Moscow. He has international experience as visiting scholar to institutions such as the IMF and the Bank of Finland. He has published extensively, both in Russia and internationally, and is concluding a book on the Russian economy and the new economic strategy, co-authored with Niclas Sundström.

Peter M. Halloran. *Executive chairman, Aton Capital Group, president of Pharos.* Peter M. Halloran is the founder of Pharos Russia Advisors Ltd. Pharos was established in 1997 has been an active investor in equity, private equity and fixed-income opportunities in Russia and the CIS. Pharos has also acted as an outside advisor to portfolios valued in excess of $500 million. In July 2000, Peter Halloran joined the executive board of Aton Capital Group as chairman.

Since 1994, Mr Halloran has been a leading participant in the Russian market, bringing more than $7.5 billion to Russia through equity, debt and private placements. He was the principal contributor towards building the CSFB equity, fixed-income and investment banking businesses in Russia and the CIS. During his tenure, CSFB established a dominant market position as measured by trading volume, research rankings and profitability. In August 1997 he left CSFB to start Pharos Russian Advisors.

Mr Halloran has also acted as an advisor to Soros Fund Management, among others, on their activities in Russia. From 1986–95 he worked in New York for CSFB, Salomon Brothers, and CJ Lawrence, Morgan Grenfell.

He has lived in Moscow since 1995 and also maintains an office near Geneva. Mr Halloran graduated with a BA in History from Yale University in 1984.

Goohoon Kwon. *Senior sovereign strategist for emerging Europe, Middle East and Africa, ABN AMRO.* Goohoon Kwon is responsible for the formulation of fixed-income investment strategy in emerging Europe as well as economic analysis of emerging European countries both for fixed-income and equity markets at ABN AMRO.

Dr Kwon worked for the IMF for five years before joining ABN AMRO in mid-August 1998. At the IMF he worked on former Soviet Union countries including Russia and Ukraine as a team member and was also a resident representative in Ukraine, focusing on monetary, fiscal and structural issues. Before joining the IMF, Dr Kwon worked in Moscow to help the Russian Privatisation Ministry with its mass privatisation. He has ten years of work and research experiences on transition economies, including four years of economics Ph.D work at Harvard.

Dean LeBaron. *Chairman, Virtualquest.company, and founder, Batterymarch Financial Management.* Dean LeBaron founded Batterymarch Financial Management in 1969 and directed the firm's pioneering advances in the mid-1970s in the application of computer technology and modelling techniques, first in the US market and then in international and emerging markets. Mr LeBaron is recognized as one of the first foreign entrants in the nascent securities markets of Brazil, India, Russia and China. Today, Batterymarch is one of the investment management subsidiaries of Legg Mason Inc., which manages over $100 billion through several independently operating firms.

Prior to Batterymarch, Mr LeBaron was director of research at Keystone, where he managed the Keystone Custodian Growth Fund. He was also director of research at F.S. Moseley & Company. Mr LeBaron holds a BA and MBA from Harvard University. He received the Baker Scholar award at Harvard Business School and holds a chartered financial analyst designation (CFA). He is chairman of Wordworks Inc. In 2001 Mr LeBaron received the highest award of the Association for Investment Management and Research, the AIMR Award for Professional Excellence.

Identified as one of the investment futurists, Mr LeBaron's most recent investigations consider the development of new management styles using the Internet: virtual investment management. Inspired 15 years ago by his study of the application of physical science principles (such as quantum physics) to investment strategy, Mr LeBaron pursues his interest in complexity through *Complexity Digest* – or *ComDig* – a webzine which he publishes and through association with Santa Fe Institute and New England Complex Systems Institute and their linking of complex adaptive systems to dynamic social systems, including investments.

Drawing on input from 30 recognized experts (investment 'gurus'), Mr LeBaron has written *The Ultimate Investor* and *The Ultimate Book of Investment Quotations*. He is also the author of *Climbing Falling Walls*, recently renamed *Marx to Market*, which gives an account of market transformation in Russia and China.

Mark Mobius. *President, Templeton Emerging Markets Fund*. Mark Mobius joined Templeton in 1987 as president of Templeton Emerging Markets Fund Inc. in Hong Kong. He currently directs the analysts based in Templeton's 11 emerging markets offices and manages the emerging markets portfolios. Dr Mobius has spent over 30 years work-ing in Asia and other parts of the emerging markets world. As a result of his experience, in 1999 he was appointed joint chairman of the World Bank and OECD's Global Corporate Governance Forum's Investor Responsibility Taskforce.

In 1999, Dr Mobius was named one of the 'ten top money managers of the 20th century' in a survey by the Carson Group, a leading global capital markets intelligence-consulting firm. For the second year in a row, Dr Mobius was named the number-one global emerging market fund manager in the 1998 Reuters Survey. CNBC named him '1994 first in business money manager of the year'. Morningstar in the U.S. awarded him the 'closed-end fund manager of the year' for 1993. In 1992, Dr Mobius was named 'investment trust manager of the year' by the *Sunday Telegraph* in the United Kingdom.

Before joining Templeton, from 1983 to 1986 Dr Mobius was president of International Investment Trust Company, Taiwan's first and largest investment management firm. Prior to that, he served as a director at Vickers da Costa, an international securities firm. Before joining

Vickers, he operated his own consulting firm in Hong Kong for ten years, and was a research scientist for Monsanto Overseas Enterprises Company in Hong Kong and the American Institute for Research in Korea and Thailand.

Dr Mobius holds Bachelor and Master degrees from Boston University, and a Ph.D. in economics and political science from the Massachusetts Institute of Technology. He also studied at the University of Wisconsin, the University of New Mexico, and Kyoto University in Japan.

Dr Mobius is author of *The Investor's Guide to Emerging Markets, Mobius on Emerging Markets* and *Passport to Profits*.

Roland Nash. *Chief economist, Renaissance Capital Investment Bank.* Roland Nash has been working as an economist in Moscow for six years. He is chief economist at Renaissance Capital Investment Bank where he helps head up a research department of 11 analysts focusing on Russian assets. Before moving over to focus fully on the macroeconomic and political environment, Mr Nash ran the fixed-income credit research effort, specifically overseeing the firm's research coverage of the fledgling regional and corporate debt markets.

In the two years before joining Renaissance Capital, Mr Nash worked as an economic advisor to the Russian government with the Russian European Centre for Economic Policy in Moscow. During that period he helped develop Russia's leading macroeconomic journal, *Russian Economic Trends*.

Enrico Perotti. *Professor of International Finance, University of Amsterdam.* Enrico Perotti holds the Chair in International Finance at the University of Amsterdam. He obtained his Ph.D. in Finance from the Massachusetts Institute of Technology (MIT) in Cambridge, MA, in 1990. He has since taught courses at MIT, Boston University and the London School of Economics. He has been a visiting professor at the IMF, the London Business School and the Central European University.

Prof. Perotti's research interests are in the area of corporate finance, banking and international finance. He has written about leveraged recapitalizations, equity crosslistings, strategic real options, banking reform and regulation, comparative corporate governance, the structure of the Japanese *keiretsu*, corporate transparency, emerging market development, financial integration and political risk, privatisation and entrepreneurship. His work, both theoretical and empirical, has been published in top journals such as the *American Economic Review*, the *Journal of Financial Economics*, *The Journal of International Money and Finance*, *Management Science* and the *Journal of International Economics*. In his applied work he is an authority in the area of international corporate finance, privatisation and financial reform in emerging countries.

Prof. Perotti is director of the research centre CIFRA in Amsterdam and a Fellow of the Financial Economics and of the Transition Economics Program at CEPR, Fellow at the Davidson Institute at the University of Michigan. He has worked as a consultant for the IMF, the World Bank, the European Commission, the New York Stock Exchange, the Russian Central Bank, and the EBRD as well as various private financial institutions and Eastern European governments.

Letitia Rydjeski. *Director of emerging market investments at Strategic Fixed Income*. Letitia Rydjeski is responsible for the EU 'converging' market countries, Poland, the Czech Republic and Hungary, along with Greece and South Africa at Strategic Fixed Income in Rosslyn, Virginia. She has been involved in the former Soviet/Russian market in numerous ways since 1989.

She started her career at the Baring Securities Eastern European research desk in 1990, covering the economies and nascent equity markets of Russia, Poland, the Czech Republic and Hungary. She subsequently worked as an Eastern Europe/Russia analyst at Chemical Bank, concentrating on unrestructured, defaulted debt of Poland, Bulgaria and Russia and the debt restructurings in these countries. She also worked at Scudder, Stevens & Clark during the 'heyday' of Western investment interest in Russia, when Russia and Eastern European coverage was essential to several different funds.

Niclas Sundström. *Economic-political strategist for Russia and Eastern Europe at SSSB/Citibank*. Niclas Sundström is a Russian and East European economic-political specialist, and is economic-political strategist for Russia and Eastern Europe at Schroder Salomon Smith Barney/Citibank. Mr Sundström has a long background in the study of Russian economics, politics and the political economy of Russian economic reforms, and has co-authored several books and other published works on the Russian and East European economies. He has two new books under publication for 2001, the first with Professor Yevgeny Gavrilenkov from the Higher School of Economics in Moscow on Russian economic policy under the Putin regime, and the other with Vladimir Gligorov from the Vienna Institute of International Economic Studies on the launch of economic reforms in Yugoslavia/Serbia.

Peter Westin. *Senior economist, Aton Capital*. Peter Westin currently works as a Senior economist for ATON Capital Group in Moscow. Prior to that he worked at the Swedish think tank SITE (Stockholm Institute of Transition Economics) which spearheads international initiatives to build centres for research and policy advice in transition economies. At SITE he edited *Russian Economic Trends*, which is the world's leading publication on the Russian economy.

Peter assumed his post at SITE in July 1998, precisely when the severe financial crisis hit Russia. In this post he rapidly became one of Moscow's most sought-after commentators on the ups and downs of the economy, and regularly featured on Russian and international media programmes.

PREFACE: THE WILD EAST

ERIK BERGLOF

Referring to Russia as the 'The Wild East' has become commonplace in the financial world. It is meant to evoke images of the Wild West and the frontier civilization that has captured our imagination for more than two centuries.

The Wild West has two faces. On one hand, the dark image of crime-ridden, male-dominated towns where favourite pastimes were drinking, gambling and visits to the 'whore house'. The rule of law was embryonic at best, with physical strength and prowess with guns, rather than judges and juries, resolving conflicts. But there is also the more positive picture of the pioneers leaving their relatively secure, but desolate lives in Europe or the Eastern United States, to seek their fortunes in the open landscapes of the West. The Land of Opportunity held high risks and high returns. Settlers came to build new communities, and shaped a culture that is still with us today. There was a sense of mission: the Wild West had to be tamed through new institutions erected from scratch.

This book tells the stories of the settlers (some temporary) of the financial frontier in Russia. Our narrators have shared a common experience: as portfolio investors they observed and participated in the events that led up to the financial crisis of 1998. Some of these accounts, like their counterparts in the Wild West, have already made it into legend. Others are new, brought to us first-hand by investors who have had time to reflect on their often tumultuous experience of a few years back. To our knowledge this is the first book that brings them all together.

But hold on, some might say, many of these pioneers misjudged Russia then; why should we hear them out now? Like many settler accounts of the Wild West, these are likely to be partial and maybe even self-serving.

Moreover, why should we listen to portfolio investors at all? They often lack the on-the-ground knowledge of foreign direct investors. Portfolio investors usually come in late and leave early, and have neither the time nor the incentives to learn much about the institutions of the country. They manage large, diversified portfolios and are evaluated on short-term performance. They also tend to move in herds, suggesting that the views of the individual investor are less interesting.

Nevertheless, there are many reasons why we should listen to, even study, these accounts. While portfolio investors are sometimes less familiar with the intricacies of local institutions, they do have well-trained noses for macroeconomic and political vulnerabilities. They have broad international experience, in particular from emerging markets, giving them a rich set of comparisons. Moreover, the portfolio investors are important actors at the heart of the crisis; they *are* the short-term capital outflow. If we understand what makes portfolio investors act in certain ways, we are also closer to understanding the origin of the crisis.

And the contributors in this volume are not your average portfolio investors, either. The group, with some of the most experienced and highly regarded representatives of the profession, offers impressive combined experience. Dean LeBaron, for instance, even came to Russia during the *perestroika*. Many played important roles in the dramatic events leading up to the 1998 crisis. To the extent there was herd behaviour, these investors were among the leaders of the pack. Furthermore, not only do the stories of portfolio investors help us identify the problems; their experience can also help lead us to solutions. Several of the contributors here have participated actively in the economic decision-making process in Russia, as advisors and commentators, and occasionally as policymakers. Some have also taken part in privatisations and other important financial transactions. Many are still involved in negotiating the financial frontier in Russia and building the institutions necessary to establish the rule of law.

So why did many of the authors here seem to have seriously misjudged Russia? Their own answers in this volume suggest that it was the lack of understanding of the weaknesses of local institutions, in particular the poor protection of minority investors, that hurt them in Russia. Economic research has borne out this lesson: work by Simon Johnson and three co-authors suggests that it was precisely the differences in the rule of law and minority protection, not the macro-imbalances and indebtedness, that explained why some countries were hit by the Asian Crisis and others not. But more recent findings also imply that many observers did not fully appreciate the implicit contingent liabilities of the governments in these countries. In Russia these liabilities originated in a bloated market for government bonds and a fundamentally defunct banking system saddled with large amounts of bad debts and huge exposures in markets for foreign exchange and bonds.

There is also much to suggest that the crises we see today are different from those of the past, a factor that helps to explain why the portfolio investors may not have anticipated the Russian crisis. Financial and economic crises are more contagious than they were during earlier periods of high capital mobility. The new crisis pathologies provide yet another reason for why we should listen carefully to the voices in this volume.

Another related issue is that some portfolio investors, like Letitia Rydjeski, did have serious concerns but did not heed these. This leads to the deeper issue of *why* portfolio investors, and investors in general, move in herds. As Al Breach confides, 'it is hard to remove yourself from the crowd'. Obviously, in the financial industry incentives matter. It is more costly to be wrong alone than in a crowd. But there are also more subtle psychological factors that cause us to doubt our own judgement. This is the exciting new area of behavioural finance, which is rapidly changing our understanding of financial markets and institutions.

But did these portfolio investors really misjudge Russia? To quote Al Breach, they seemed to have been 'fooled' not once but twice. Many with money in the market held their positions too long, and sold too early, before the upturn. But was this serious misjudgement, or just simple calculation? Those investors that did not manage to sell before August 1998 lost money relative to the peak of the boom. But to know whether they lost money we need to know when they entered and at what prices. Those who bought equity did so in a heavily discounted market, in some stocks by a factor of a hundred. These prices reflected fundamental concerns about the lack of institutions and macroeconomic imbalances in Russia. Others loaded up on government securities at unbelieveable interest rates, several hundred per cent on a yearly basis right before the crisis reaching 135 per cent on average in August 1998. Obviously, these rates incorporated the possibility of default. Experienced investors that bought in these markets knew what they were getting into. The risks were huge but so were the potential rewards.

In investment, timing is, if not everything, at least very important. While the collapse in August 1998 could not have been a surprise to most of these investors, the upturn in 1999 and 2000 seems to have been. Most observers had anticipated that the impact of a financial crisis on the real sector would be limited, after all very few firms relied on credits from the financial sector. It was also obvious to most that a depreciation of the rouble would give an impetus to many industries. But very few observers expected such broad and rapid growth. Manufacturing has grown by a third in three years; industries previously pronounced dead were revived, and parts of the country that had contracted for decades suddenly showed signs of life. The world oil price has helped substantially, but it only explains part of the development. After the crisis, Russia has experienced a period of renewed political vigour and ambitious reform plans; the federal state has reasserted itself. Limited progress has already been made in tax reform and administrative simplification. Critical judicial reform is now on the agenda.

Yet the vulnerabilities remain. The frontier of the Wild East, like its counterpart in the American West, is not always well-defined and does not always move forward. Negotiating the financial frontier in Russia is a long and arduous process where no gains of terrain are ever secure. The Phoenix rising out of the ashes of the Russian financial sector may have shorter wings and less vigour. This may prevent it from flying as high as it did in 1998, thus making a plunge less dramatic, but another crisis in the near future cannot be ruled out. The banking sector has not been restructured, and the rules of the game in the financial sector are far from clear. The supervisory bodies lack bite and the Central Bank and its governor, previously branded for not believing in the relationship between money and inflation, are now ignoring all international experience on bank restructuring. If nothing serious is done about the Russian banks, we may well see an eerie rerun of the 1998 crisis with an overvalued rouble and an extremely fragile and bloated banking sector.

This is one reason to be cautious about the prospects for Russian economic reforms, and there are others. The government has an ambitious reform programme, and President Putin has increasingly put his weight behind it. It is by far the most comprehensive programme to date in Russia and local ownership is stronger than it has ever been. But the programme lacks clear priorities. Together with Club 2015, a group of young Russian business leaders and policymakers, SITE and our Russian-born offspring CEFIR are trying to assist the government in setting these priorities. Transparency and broad public debate are critical to this process. In a project with the Ministry of Economic Development and Trade, and with support from the World Bank, we are developing a programme for monitoring implementation of the programme at the level of the individual enterprise. It is only when the reality facing the individual entrepreneur improves that we can hope for sustained economic growth in Russia.

Like the old frontier towns of the West, Russia has yet to establish the very foundation upon which 'rule of law' must be built: a strong, competent and fiscally sound state with clear demarcations towards special interests, and contained corruption. The problem of Russia is not an absence of laws on the book; it is enforcement of these laws. A combination of institutional reform and stronger norms helped to build the foundations for a stronger state and an unprecedented period of sustainable economic growth in the Wild West. For Russia this is the ultimate challenge.

Learning from foreign experience, and the experience of foreign investors, is important, but genuine progress will only come once the analysis and its conclusions have been internalized. Building domestic analytical capacity through a reversal of the brain drain and stronger domestic training is critical to a sustainable reform process. To this construction SITE is committed.

Erik Berglöf

Stockholm, 17 July 2001

PART I

Exploring the wilderness

1

BANKING REGULATION IN A CONTEXT OF EXTREME LEGAL UNDERDEVELOPMENT: LESSONS FROM THE RUSSIAN MELTDOWN

ENRICO PEROTTI

THE SCALE AND SCOPE OF THE RUSSIAN public debt and banking collapse of 1998, not to mention its speed, offered a dramatic example of the problems in constructing a decentralized financial system in countries with limited experience of market mechanisms.[1] We will argue that much can be learned from this experience. There is an argument that Russia is a 'special case' because of its size, complexity and history. However, our experience makes us believe that Russia is not unique, and that its citizens do not have a different system of economic preferences and aspirations compared with other countries. Quite simply, Russia is a large example of the systemic consequences of a structure of individual incentives built on a weak legal environment.

Russia's fall was spectacular largely because its reform effort had been long and strongly supported, for political reasons, by international financial institutions, both directly (via a large amount of International Monetary Fund (IMF), World Bank and OECD (Organization for Economic Co-operation and Development) government lending) and by the implicit guarantees that foreign investors saw in the direct support provided by the West. This allowed a longer run before this particular experiment – of an externally supported macro-stabilization policy in a largely unreformed legal and microeconomic context – finally crashed. Most other countries are not usually allowed such a long run, and their failures are therefore less spectacular. Arguably, a longer and deeper experience, such as that of Russia, can help understand the flaws in the conventional approach to other countries.

While the institutional problems that Russia faced were present in varying degrees in all transition countries, there is in fact a larger set of economies in which a proper financial system has failed to emerge. There is a consensus that this deficiency is the result of serious weakness of the legal and institutional framework, as in Russia's case. It is less clear what we should understand to be such a weakness. Since there is by now a consensus on the crucial role of institutions, it is imperative to be clear on what we mean by institutional weakness.

Here we present a view of the underlying structure of individual incentives in the Russian crisis, and interpret the events and trends leading into the crisis as a result of such incentives.

AN INTERPRETATIVE MODEL OF FINANCIAL BEHAVIOUR FOR THE RUSSIAN ECONOMY

We will put forward two basic moral hazard structures, one based on individual incentives (micro) and one based on collective collusive incentives. To understand the nature of this behaviour we will first restate what is by now a consensus view, namely that economic decisions and transactions in Russia are not generally constrained by laws and contractual obligations *per se* because enforcement is unreliable (that is, it can be bought off by either party). As a result, settlement and compliance are a matter of almost pure bargaining. Rules and agreement are as binding as the strength of the bargaining counterpart. For paradoxical illustration, the effectiveness of widespread criminal preying on legal activities shows that enforcement may be best in uncontracted circumstances. Because of this lack of rules, control rights are extremely valuable – much more valuable than contractual titles. In fact, the key to decision making is operational control rather than formal ownership. So what form of behaviour by those in control will flourish in such an environment?

The 1992–4 privatization and financial liberalization notionally created private institutions, via insider privatization and entry of new banks. The first question is whether there was an incentive to restructure enterprises or build up strong institutions, and the answer now appears to be clear.

Insider privatization brought neither new managerial nor financial resources to enterprises. The old management gained explicit control, often by buying worker shares or by creating insider share blocks. The value of this control, namely the right to manoeuvre and manipulate assets, was greater than what they could hope to gain by selling out shares of the loss-making enterprise to external investors. The incentive was to transform control over assets into personal wealth while escaping prosecution and taxation (from the state or from criminals). Liquidity of assets here was crucial, as a safe appropriation required an easy transfer. This generated an overwhelming cash-stripping incentive. Assets were swapped at arbitrary prices for cash, which could be easily diverted (and often joined the capital flight to safe foreign accounts). Even moderate estimates of capital flight from Russia put the amount at over two times total IMF lending, with the balance largely reflecting under-invoicing by exporters.

The consequences of cash-stripping reverberate well beyond the enterprise sphere. Cash settlements gradually became a rarity, as all managers tried to hoard cash. Trade credit rapidly turned into arrears once stabilization policy started in 1992. After each tightening phase arrears exploded, rapidly dwarfing bank credit, and forcing two partial bailouts in 1992 and 1993. Afterwards trade credit largely stopped. Barter, which had a long tradition under Soviet central planning, became a necessity to maintain essential exchanges with other firms.[2]

Barter was a sustainable form of exchange because significant suppliers and customers had longstanding relationships and mutual bargaining power, and because it did not create any strong incentive to strip cash. The main avenue for retaining cash was to run up arrears with anyone too weak to bargain. Non-payment to banks depended much on the nature of the loan. Anecdotal evidence suggests that smaller or uncon-nected firms had little chance of bank credit, and when they did receive loans they rarely dared to delay payment (unless forced to do so by a liquidity shortage, due in turn to non-payment). At the same time, connected lending (loans to insiders and friends) was often either extremely underpriced or was in fact an outright transfer – the cash would be lent to a shell firm, which would ultimately vanish, leaving no trace of its real owners.

In contrast, wage arrears rose astronomically, since *de facto* wages had the lowest seniority of all claims. In no other industrialized country have workers suffered such a degree of non-payment with such resignation.[3] Liabilities to the tax authorities were next to wages at the bottom of the seniority league. Of course, the ability to resist tax payment depended much on the enterprise's size and its political strength (often related to local government connections). However, the tax arrears game quickly grew on the strength, once again, of a collective collusive game.

66In no other industrialized country have workers suffered such a degree of non-payment with such resignation99

Consider the incentive of a Russian firm with some cash and large tax liabilities and consider its incentive to delay payment. There may be some costs due to the risk of strong enforcement measures. This risk is likely to diminish as the number of firms in arrears increases, since the tax authorities face an ever harder task to collect their money. So the perceived risk reflects the perception of what other firms are doing. There were financial penalties for late tax payment (often quite severe penalties), but final settlement was almost always a matter of bargaining.

Consider next the incentive to delay payment, represented by the yield on liquid investment (such as GKOs). The lower the tax revenues, the larger the budget gap and the need to issue bonds, the higher the yield on GKOs. Thus the costs of delay fell and its rewards rose as a function of the perceived number of firms in tax arrears. Even the firm's bargaining strength regarding settlement was likely to be affected by the degree of delay. Political changes, which were seen as weakening of the centre, could have a disproportionate effect on tax compliance if they became a focal point for expectations of a weaker bargaining position by the federal government.

The other sector where cash stripping was easy and widespread was banking. In the early years of reform, minimum capital requirements for a banking licence were ridiculously low and monitoring was lax. The number of Russian banks went from less than ten to almost 3000 in a few years. Banks made money speculating against the rouble and sitting on transfer payment for long periods while earning the float. Many banks were legal boxes rather than credit institutions with a long-term strategy: generated cash flow was taken out while liabilities were kept in the box. The sector was chronically and deliberately undercapitalized, and capital increases required by later regulation were often achieved by owners using funds borrowed from the bank itself.

The number of banks declined slightly under the regulatory tightening of Tatyana Paramonova, then acting chairman of the Central Bank of Russia (CBR), who followed a more rigorous monetary policy. The more obvious short-term players (pure pyramid schemes such as MMM) went under. However, the number of banks remained excessive in relation to the amount of legitimate proper investment. While this reflected the fact that many banks were in fact little more than finance companies for firms and individuals, in general the degree of competition around better lending meant that conventional banking activity was not attractive relative to whitewashing, lobbying and speculation.

The best-connected banks attracted the balances of state authorities, and top bankers even sat in the government. The pinnacle of opportunism was reached with the famous loans-for-shares transactions of 1995–6, which elegantly transferred ownership of controlling blocks in handpicked cash-rich oil and natural resource companies to banks as the predictable result of collateralized loans to the government. In the roaring days of 1994 the government had become convinced that Russia needed Japanese-style *keiretsu*, and loans for shares created them in the form of FIGs (financial-industrial groups), a Russian version of *keiretsu*, in which banks run groups of large industrial firms in need of long-term investment.

The experience of these groups is highly controversial. Groups are common in underdeveloped financial systems, and it is often claimed that they provide governance and an internal capital market to firms which would otherwise be credit-constrained. Research on bank-controlled FIGs has shown that cash flows from cash-rich firms in the groups were reallocated on a massive scale. While to some extent this may have reflected shifting of funds towards better investment opportunities within the group (investment in group firms is correlated with their Tobin's Q, unlike non-group firms), the scale of the reallocation suggests opportunistic transfers as well.[4]

In the progressive stabilization of 1996–7, inflation fell and the rouble appreciated in real terms. Banks, which survived the loss of speculative gains from speculating on the dollar, benefited from the declining attractiveness of 'mattress' dollar savings for the population. A gradual restoration of confidence (the Russian stock market was a global top performer in 1997) led to some increase in money demand in the form of rouble and dollar deposits. The Russian state had stopped funding its deficit by monetary emission and switched to issue of rouble bonds (GKOs). The GKO market started life offering fantastic yields to authorized banks, motivating them to gather retail savings. In 1997, as yields dropped (in part, as foreigners became heavily involved), there were even signs of increased interest by banks in lending to the real economy. This trend, whether healthy or not, was rapidly reversed as uncertainty and volatility rose on all emerging markets following the early signs of the Asian crisis. The final stage of the prolonged Ponzi game represented by the GKO market was beginning.

In this final stage, banks lost all interest in lending and threw themselves into speculation. The short-term returns were excellent as long as the rouble peg held. As GKO rates rose in late 1997, foreigners bought massive amounts of forward coverage from the main Russian banks. These zero-investment bets by the banks generated rich cash flows, paying a significant part of the interest rate differential on the notional capital at each contract expiration. The gains were increasingly shifted abroad while new exposure was created on the bank balance sheet. Nominally, this exposure was covered by secondary hedges made with secondary Russian banks, whose chances of solvency in the case of a rouble fall were nil. The amount of contingent liabilities soon dwarfed not just bank capital but also bank assets in order of magnitude. While banks could formally argue that their net exposure was small, the unreliability of side hedges meant that the exposure was in fact close to its gross figure.

It is likely that bankers bet the bank on the short-term return on rouble investments while persistently shifting cash flow gained from short-term bets to foreign private accounts. While it may be argued that the CBR condoned certain practices in an attempt to protect the rouble, it is also true that the banking system was allowed to pile up immense exposure while maintaining minimal capital. The incentive was to siphon out cash, leaving formal institutions as liability shells.[5]

> **❝The amount of contingent liabilities soon dwarfed not just bank capital but also bank assets in order of magnitude.❞**

In the end, both the banking system and the government debt market were run as Ponzi schemes. The persistent failure to collect taxes was the result of cash-extracting incentives from tax-collecting institutions or the ability of too many enterprises to resist enforcement, aided by local politicians and a snowball effect. As in all pyramid schemes, their short-term stability required steady inflows, which western investors and institutions provided. It is telling to compare the overall numbers. The IMF lent around $20 billion to Russia, while other private and public institutions lent another $80 billion. Russia's estimated stock of capital flight in the decade was $130 billion.

CONCLUSION

The Russian stabilization programme failed because its macroeconomic logic was predicated on a different structure of incentives than that offered by the real legal and political context. Aggregate restrictive policies failed to affect individual behaviour, not because they demanded too much too soon, as many have concluded, but because the political foundations allowed more powerful or better-connected individuals to escape responsibility for their actions, and more generally, created collective incentives for opportunistic behaviour.

Is Russia different from other countries? What is the role of its culture? We believe that Russians are driven by the same ambitions as any other culture. Yet Russians have a different set of expectations of what other (Russians) will do, and the role of these expectations is central in any systemic transition. Russians often acted opportunistically because they expected other Russians to do the same – clearly, no law can be enforced when a majority of individuals ignore it. Thus illegal behaviour becomes a rational individual strategy, which in the end is validated by collective behaviour. Yet the bad example in Russia often came from the top. Compared with other countries, political power in Russia was too unconstrained by institutional checks and balances.

Notes

[1] This article summarizes my interpretation of the perverse, if rational, behaviour in the Russian financial system. I spent two-and-a-half years as a policy advisor to the Russian government and the Central Bank, under a project funded by the EU's TACIS programme.

[2] Barter had a long tradition in Soviet times. In addition, barter made it possible to escape taxation, and may have served to strip assets or exchange favours. In fact, the very emergence of barter destroys information about valuation by leaving no common unit for accounting.

[3] At the same time, unpaid wages were sometimes a useful argument for delaying tax payments to authorities.

[4] Along with the hierarchical bank-dominated groups, other FIGs were created around trade associations. These groups had no central control structure but were horizontal industrial alliances for the purpose of joint lobbying, mutual support and cartelization. While few of the announced tax advantages were actually granted, many FIGs benefited from informal favours and market power.

[5] A historical parallel can be drawn here with the old story of the corrupt governor sent by the czar to manage tax collection and local administration in a far-away province, and who whistled away all the revenues. When the czar announced that he would send a representative to examine the results of his administration, the governor rushed to have wooden palace façades built in front of all the decrepit buildings in the neglected central boulevard. He then joined the czar's representative who drove down the street in a coach admiring the thriving city architecture.

2

RUSSIA'S INVESTMENT ADVENTURE: BUYING IN OR BAILING OUT?

PETER WESTIN[1]

INTRODUCTION

CAPITAL INFLOWS HAVE PLAYED AN IMPORTANT ROLE in the reform process in Central and Eastern Europe, and will continue to do so for some time. The initial lack of indigenous funds, coupled with deterioration of the existing capital stock, means that foreign investments, loans and aid can make a huge difference in providing strong support for economic growth. However, countries' ability to attract external funds is largely dependent on their progress with reform. The more advanced economies of Central Europe have, not surprisingly, been able to attract more investments. In this respect the choice of privatisation strategy also makes a difference. Countries that chose to restructure enterprises before selling them, such as Hungary and later Poland, were able to charge a higher price for their assets than countries that chose to privatize first and restructure later. Countries in the latter group, including Russia, more or less had to 'give away' their state-owned enterprises.

Capital flows to emerging markets were severely hit first by the Asian crisis in 1997 and then by the Russian crisis in 1998, shortly followed by financial turmoil in Brazil in early 1999. These upsets coincided with a period when markets in Europe and the United States were experiencing higher growth rates, thus attracting more attention from investors compared with emerging markets. Gross private financing to emerging markets fell sharply from $292.5 billion in 1997 to $150.2 billion in 1998, recovering somewhat in 1999 to $173.2 billion. Capital flows to Asia were most affected, but flows to Central and Eastern Europe were also severely hit, falling by two-thirds in the period 1998–9. Russia accounted for nearly all of this decline, while capital flows to more advanced countries in the region remained more stable. Furthermore, the flow of foreign direct investment (FDI) remained more stable than the flow of portfolio investments. Portfolio investments, often referred to as 'hot money', are, by nature, more mobile and therefore will rapidly seek a safer or more profitable host country when a crisis appears. FDI is more often related to a long-term investment strategy of foreign multinational enterprises, bringing in fixed capital, know-how related to management, marketing and organisational skills.

Russia's ability to attract foreign investments should be huge, with its vast deposits of natural resources, market size, highly educated workforce, and significant growth potential. However, this ability will be realized only if reforms aimed at improving the investment and general business climate in Russia are given priority. The current Russian leadership has expressed commitment to this aim.

CONDITIONS AND BENEFITS OF INVESTMENTS

Investments can bring large benefits to the host country, as well as to the investor. For transition economies, the progress of reform remains the main key to attracting FDI. Creating a good investment climate does not only involve macroeconomic stability but also progress at the micro level as well as institutional reforms such as privatisation, restructuring, and legal and taxation frameworks. For the host country foreign investments can compensate for shortfalls in domestic investments, and also create spill-over effects. The latter occur when foreign companies make use of domestic financial institutions and distribution networks, or when new (supporting) businesses are created as a consequence of the investment. In addition, foreign investments provide the country with know-how, particularly management and organisational skills. Although it is clear that a successful investment climate created by market-oriented reforms is important for attracting investments, investments themselves can help to push reforms forward. This is especially true with regard to enterprise restructuring, as foreign investments contribute to the creation of market institutions, e.g. more stringent legal requirements and improved enterprise behaviour. They can also foster competition among domestic producers.

As regards motives for FDI investors, the current trend is a reduction in importance of the cost motive, i.e. relocating production to a country with lower production costs. Other factors, such as market access, market share, and proximity to the European Union (EU) and the Central European Free Trade Area (CEFTA), are more important determinants of investor interest in the post-communist economies. Also, it was clear early on that some of the CEE countries would seek EU membership, making them more attractive as investment hosts than countries that are set to remain outside the EU.

Different approaches to privatisation in the various transition countries have been crucial in attracting or discouraging foreign investments. Mass privatisation *à la* Russia and the Czech Republic, in which previously state-owned assets were more or less given away, meant that restructuring of these enterprises was postponed, only to become a headache for the new owner. A serious effort to sell assets at the highest price, as in Hungary, means that restructuring has to take place before the sale, making the assets more attractive for foreign investors. It is critical for the privatisation process to be fair and transparent. Obviously, it is also critical that the privatisation rules should clearly allow foreigners to buy the assets on offer. Foreigners could not participate in the first Russian privatisation wave, which ended in the summer of 1994. As the second wave started, in which strategic enterprises were put up for sale, domestic interest groups crowded out foreign participation, mainly via the 'loans-for-shares' scheme. This created poor initial conditions for foreign investments in Russia.

> **Different approaches to privatisation in the various transition countries have been crucial in attracting or discouraging foreign investments.**

FEATURES OF FOREIGN INVESTMENT IN RUSSIA
....

Figure 2.1, presenting quarterly flows of portfolio and direct foreign investments to Russia from 1994 to the end of 2000, tells an interesting story about foreign investors and their *modus operandi*, as well as about Russia, 'the commodity'. Portfolio investors coming to a risky environment naturally look for shares with large growth prospects and other securities offering high returns. Foreign direct investors, on the other hand, are basing investment decisions on issues such as market

Figure 2.1 *Quarterly net flows of foreign investments to Russia, 1994–2000*

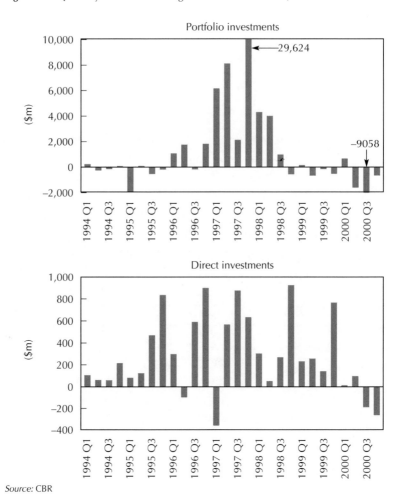

Source: CBR

size, first-mover considerations, and relative production costs, e.g. labour. As FDI normally involves a long-term investment strategy, the economic situation and the business and investment climate in the host country play a larger role than for portfolio investments.

Between 1994 and 2000 net portfolio investments amounted to $44.9 billion. The pattern of portfolio investment in Russia during this period shows that there was a sudden upsurge from the end of 1996 to the second quarter of 1998, and this despite no real improvements in the investment climate. The upsurge was driven by huge returns on government securities and a booming stock market. In order to finance its large budget deficit the government issued bonds, and in order to attract investors, both domestic and foreign, the risky environment had to be compensated by high returns, which at times were close to or even above 100 per cent in real terms.

Foreigners were kept out of the GKO market in the early days, although foreign money would have brought down interest rates and reduced the burden of debt-service payments. During this period, the volume of the GKO market expanded from zero to $40 billion. The excessive interest rates on this debt amounted to a transfer from future taxpayers (or, as it has turned out, from investors who were defaulted on) to banks and bankers. From 1994 the amount of primary deficit financing performed by GKOs was about $15 billion. By the end of July 1998 the market was worth $70 billion in nominal terms. That difference of $55 billion was simply interest to investors, most of which went to the domestic banking sector.

Russia's relatively young stock market also experienced a bonanza in 1996 and 1997, with the RTS index growing by 142 per cent and 98 per cent respectively. In both years Russia had one of the best-performing stock markets in the world. High oil prices and belief that Russian shares remained highly undervalued attracted investor interest.

However, after the August 1998 crisis and the default by the government on its securities, portfolio investors withdrew completely (see Figure 2.1). A sudden surge in inflation pushed interest rates back into negative territory and the stock market plummeted. Suddenly, the opportunities for 'hot money' gains had disappeared. It became clear that it would take a long time for private-sector finance to regain trust in the Russian government and be ready to provide financing. Portfolio investment has yet to recover, and when it does Western institutional investors will obviously be more cautious.

Figure 2.2 *Real interest rate on GKOs during the 'investmnet boom'*

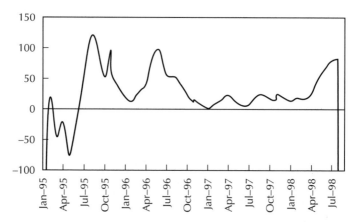

Source: CBR, RECEP, RTS

Figure 2.3 *The stock market 1995–2001*

Source: CBR, RECEP, RTS

Although profit margins are high and there are many opportunities for profitable investments, the climate facing economic actors clearly is still not sufficiently hospitable to cater for larger inflows. Russia 'the commodity' is very good, but the packaging and marketing need significant improvement. The trend in flows of foreign direct investments confirms this. Because of its bumpy reform process and volatile investment climate Russia has received one of the lowest levels of FDI of all post-communist countries. Between 1994 and 2000 a mere $19 billion of FDI came to Russia ($7.7 billion net FDI). Russia has received just $53 accumulated FDI per capita. This compares with $1900 per capita for Hungary, $1500 for the Czech Republic, and $1250 for Estonia.[2] Only four transition countries of 26 have received a lower level of FDI per capita than Russia (Belarus, Tajikistan, Ukraine, and Uzbekistan). Equally, the level of FDI has been staggeringly low as a percentage of gross domestic product (GDP). Since 1994 (when the CBR started reporting FDI on a balance-of-payment basis), the level of net FDI has remained below 1 per cent of GDP.

The net inflow of FDI has remained more stable than portfolio investments. This is especially true for the period 1995–9 (at an extremely low level), with only a slight dip following the 1998 crisis. However, in 2000 the net inflow was negative for the first time as direct investments by Russian companies abroad reached $3 billion as a result of larger profits due to the increasingly favourable economic situation and high oil prices. Despite excellent economic results in 2000 and the noticeable commitment of the authorities to reform, investors continue to adopt a wait-and-see policy towards Russia.

RUSSIA'S INVESTMENT CLIMATE

The low levels of investments that have flowed into Russia are a response to its lack of reform and thus to its inadequate investment climate, led by an obscure legal environment, including lack of protection of private property right and of small shareholders, as well as a lack of contract enforcement.

The European Bank of Reconstruction and Development (EBRD) produces an index, which sets out to estimate the state of reforms in Central and Eastern Europe. By correlating these with inflow of net foreign investments per capita (in this case foreign direct investments) for 26 transition countries, one can see that a clear relationship exists

Figure 2.4 *The stage of reforms and level of FDI per capita in Central and Eastern Europe*

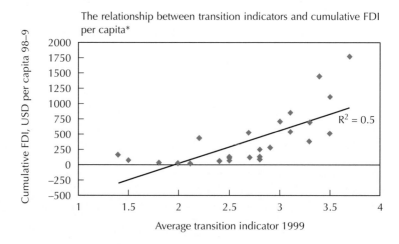

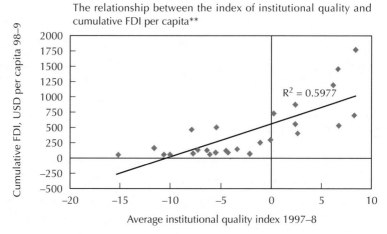

Source: EBRD, Wader, B. (2000) *Institutional Reform in Transition Economies: How Far Have They Come?* IMF (unpublished).

* Cumulative FDI up to 1999, and the average transition index for 26 Central and East European countries for 1999.
** Cumulative FDI up to 1999 and the average index of institutional quality in 1997–8 for 26 Central and East European countries. *The Index of Institutional Quality* (Wader, 2000) ranges from –25 to +25, and the average value for advanced industrial economies is 12.6.

between the stage of reforms and the amount of investments these countries have been able to attract (Figure 2.4). Countries such as Hungary, the Czech Republic and Poland that have made significant progress in reforming their economies have, not surprisingly, been able to attract more FDI. Another index, which highlights the quality of institutions, based on expert opinions from commercial risk-rating agencies and other organizations, as well as surveys of firms and households, gives a similar picture. Structural and institutional reforms are clearly vital for attracting foreign investments.

A closer look at the EBRD's transition indicators shows the development of reforms in Russia and consequences for the investment climate. Figure 2.5. shows development of the overall reform indicator, and one can see that slow improvements were made up to 1997 but that the August 1998 crisis led to a setback for reform lasting into 1999. A breakdown of the components (Figures 2.6 to 2.8.) reveals the source of this development.

❝Feeble efforts at restructuring enterprises and creating a decent structure of corporate governance have been heavily criticized throughout Russia's reform period.❞

The liberalization of trade and foreign exchange rate systems experienced the most significant setback as the CBR introduced a number of currency regulations after the crisis, some of which are still in place. Equally, both banking reform and the formation of securities markets decelerated. In the aftermath of the crisis most of Russia's banks were *de facto* bankrupt, and initiated a process of stripping whatever 'good' assets they had left, with creditors absorbing most of the losses and with little action taken by the CBR. The crisis and default on GKOs also meant that Russia's securities markets became more or less moribund, with a negative effect on development of, for example, the framework for issuance of securities by enterprises and other aspects of the regulatory framework for brokers and other market-makers.

Feeble efforts at restructuring enterprises and creating a decent structure of corporate governance have been heavily criticized throughout Russia's reform period. In 1999 the situation deteriorated further, with clear signs of weak enforcement of bankruptcy legislation and weak

Figure 2.5 *Russia's overall reform progress 1994–2000**

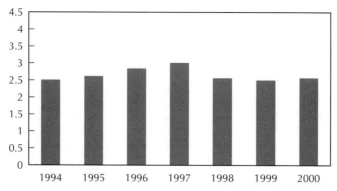

Source: EBRD

* The transition indicators produced by the EBRD range from 1 to 4+, where 1 represents little or no progress in reforming the post-communist economy and 4+ represents a standard that would be found in an industrialized market economy. For a thorough explanation of these indicators, see *Transition Report 2000* (EBRD). The author has, for the purpose of presenting these indicators in full numeric form, re-denominated these indicators in such manner that e.g. 3– equals 2.67 and 3+ equals 3.33. Thus 4+ (a standard that would be found in an industrialised market economy) is equal to 4.33.

Figure 2.6 *Russia's reform progress – enterprise (1994–2000)*

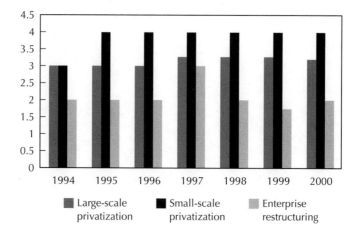

Figure 2.7 *Russia's reform progress – Markets and trade (1994–2000)*

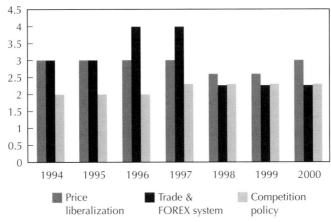

Source: EBRD

Figure 2.8 *Russia's reform progress – financial institutions (1994–2000)*

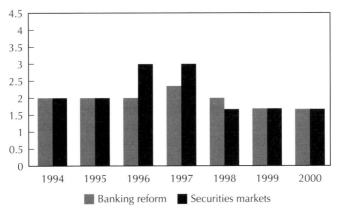

Source: EBRD

financial discipline. In order to be able to attract interest from investors (foreign as well as domestic), enterprise restructuring and improvements in corporate governance are perhaps the most crucial challenges facing Russian policymakers today. It is unclear to what extent the favourable post-crisis economic environment – created by the devaluation and high commodity prices – has actually had a negative impact on further reforms in this area, but clearly tough reform decisions are easier to make when times are 'bad'. It is easier to postpone harsh and unpopular decisions during 'good times'.

The legal environment

A favourable investment climate has to be supported by the rule of law, supporting a good corporate governance structure and contract enforcement.[3] Studies have shown that the determinants for corporate finance and governance can be related to the legal environment. Other studies have shown that high legal standards are positively correlated with dispersed ownership and relatively liquid capital markets.[4] Thus, in a country where shareholder rights are protected, investors can afford to take a minority position rather than a controlling stake. Furthermore, firm structure and stock market development have been shown to be related to the quality of shareholder protection.[5]

Figure 2.9 presents the EBRD's indicators for the process of legal reforms in Russia during the period 1998–2000, more specifically commercial law (a) and financial regulations (b). Using the same scale of measurement as in Figure 2.5, where 4.33 (originally 4+) represents the legal standard to be found in a developed market economy, a distinction is made between the overall status of legal reform, its extensiveness and its effectiveness. Extensiveness refers to the development of the actual legal text, while effectiveness has to be considered the most important aspect of legal reforms, as it indicates to what extent laws are clear and accessible, and whether they are actually enforced – the fact that laws are passed and on the statute book is meaningless unless they are actually implemented.

Figure 2.9 *Russia's progress on reforming its legal system 1998–2000**

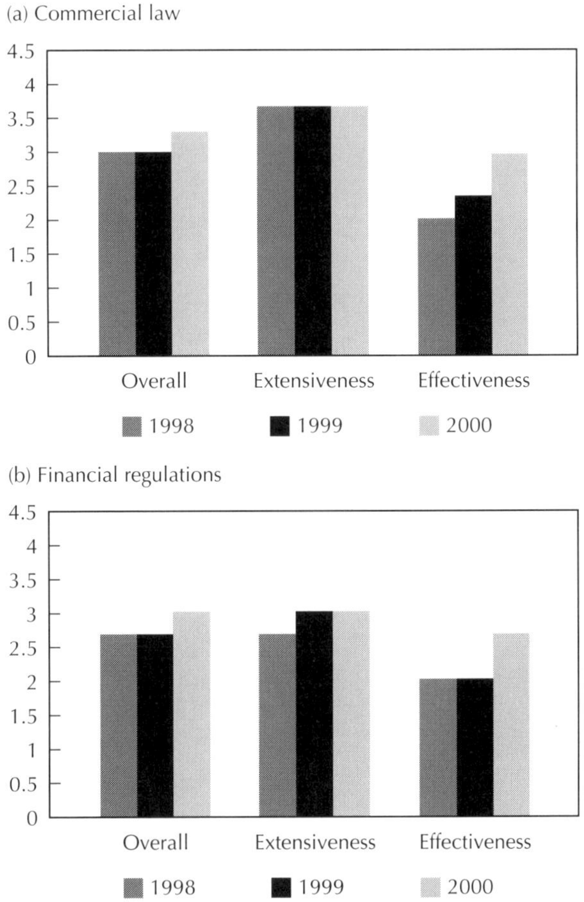

(a) Commercial law

1998   1999   2000

(b) Financial regulations

1998   1999   2000

Source: EBRD

* The legal indicators produced by the EBRD range from 1 to 4+, where 1 represents little or no progress in reforming the post-communist legal environment and 4+ represents a standard that would be found in an industrialzsed market economy. For a thorough explanation of these indicators, see *Transition Report 2000* (EBRD). The author has, for the purpose of presenting these indicators in full numeric form, re-denominated these indicators in such manner that e.g. 3– equals 2.67 and 3+ equals 3.33. Thus 4+ (the legal standard that would be found in an industrialised market economy) is equal to 4.33.

Commercial law

Russian commercial law (including bankruptcy and company law) is, on paper, close to what one can find in Western economies. This is especially true for Russian company law. Nevertheless, application and implementation fall short, although there have been some improvements since the 1998 crisis, according to the EBRD. Two aspects of Russian commercial law continue to create particular obstacles for investors. Existing legislation does not ensure adequate corporate governance or adequate protection of shareholder rights. Related to this is the issue of security of ownership that has materialized from Russia's earlier privatisation. Currently, a privatisation deal can be cancelled within ten years of its conclusion, creating enough instability and uncertainty to discourage investments. Calls have been made to reduce this to one year.

Second, contract enforcement in Russia is still inadequate. Effective contract enforcement is crucial to a country's investment climate. The underdeveloped court system means that contracting, to a larger extent, is based on relationships between parties, but also, relational contracting can act as a substitute for the court.[6] However, ability to rely on a well-developed court system would give firms more freedom to abandon existing relationships (partners) in favour of new, lower-priced ones, thus nurturing market developments and competition, and improving the investment climate.

Financial regulations

While Russia's banking system was more or less bankrupt after the crisis in August 1998, two-and-a-half years later most banks were making profits. However, almost nothing had been done to reform the sector. Restructuring of the largest failed banks was and is extremely slow and inconsistent. The CBR withdrew many banks' licences. But in spite of this, the number of banks has remained more or less stable since August 1998.

Financial regulation assesses banking and capital market laws, where a benchmark is provided by the Basle Committee on Banking Supervision's Core Principles. As with commercial law, extensiveness has developed further than effectiveness. Russia is facing both internal and external pressure to speed up reforms in its banking sphere, where there has still been little progress. Before the crisis, the banking system did not fulfil an important role as intermediary between savers and investors or as a channel for payment transactions (a vital mechanism for sustainable economic growth). Instead the real economy 'survived' by using barter and running up arrears. As use of barter and arrears have diminished in the post-crisis environment, the importance for the business community of having a bona fide banking system is increasing.

Externally, multilateral organizations such as the IMF, the World Bank and the EBRD are stressing the need for banking reforms. Nevertheless, there is still no clear consensus on how to carry out reform, still less on how to regulate the state and non-state banking system. There are still 1300 banks operating in Russia, but the strategy of both the government and the CBR seems to be to strengthen the role of state banks (the reverse strategy from that in most other transition countries). In fact, an additional three state banks have been created in the past year. The experience of other countries shows that increased dominance by the state sector has a negative effect on financial sector development, productivity and economic growth.

The *de facto* monopoly of Sberbank (the Central Bank-owned savings bank) is partly explained by an unofficial state guarantee of its private deposits. There is, therefore, an urgent need to adopt and implement a law on deposit insurance to put other banks on an equal footing and thus nurture competition. However, the authorities are faced with a dilemma: by introducing a general state deposit insurance scheme before an effective and manageable system of supervisory practice has been implemented would be associated with a high degree of fiscal risk.

66Laws on collateral and insolvency are toothless, so it is hard to make use of enforceable contracts.99

Equally, further improvements need to be made regarding creditor protection. Laws on collateral and insolvency are toothless, so it is hard to make use of enforceable contracts. Also, the issue of money laundering, which culminated in 1999 with the Bank of New York scandal, has to be dealt with and relevant legislation has to be adopted and implemented. At present there is no law in Russia dealing with the legalization of illegal incomes. As a result, the reputation of Russian banks in the West has deteriorated. A related issue is that of the need for increased transparency and adoption of international accounting standards.

The issue of Russian banking renewal has a foreign investment aspect. Many transition countries, for example Poland, Hungary, the Baltic States, the Czech Republic, Bulgaria and Romania, have allowed foreign investments into their banking market. As a result, in these countries more than half of the banking system is in foreign hands, with benefits such as increased capital management know-how, and a rapid expansion of Internet banking in the Baltics and some Central European countries. In Russia the banks remain in the hands of the state and domestic companies, which in turn are controlled by a handful of individuals. So far foreign investors' interest in Russian banks has been very limited.

The authorities have promised that banking reform will finally start in 2001. The strategy is due to be adopted in September, with an emphasis on recapitalization and mergers. After three years of promises and very suspect activities within a large number of banks, it remains to be seen whether, this time round, words will be followed by action.

Red tape

Economic actors, whether they are setting up a business or investing, face a jungle of red tape in Russia, including complicated registration procedures, licensing, certification, and project approvals. For example, according to federal legislation, there are 500 economic activities that require a licence. In addition, regional governments have (illegally) introduced licensing requirements for another 600 activities. Also, up to 250 permits are needed in order to launch a construction project, and they can take from two to five years to obtain. Many of the bureaucratic obstacles facing businesses and investors are associated with an over-head cost – 'under-the-table payments' for getting round them.

A study recently conducted by Moscow State University and commissioned by the Ministry of Economic Development and Trade shows that the direct cost from red tape, often involving corruption, amounts to $7.8 billion per year or 3 per cent of GDP or 18 per cent of federal budget revenues. However, the real figure is probably twice as high. For one thing, the university study does not estimate the impact on economic growth. Furthermore, figures quoted in the mid-1990s put the total value of bribes paid by the business community at over $20 billion per year. For example, the going rate to ensure successful receipt of a government contract is estimated at 10 per cent of the total order, and the same goes for official approval of a construction project. Other anecdotal evidence, stated in the Russian press, estimates charges and bribes during investment project implementation at 10–15 per cent of the total cost.

The government is well aware of these problems and a package of legislative proposals for deregulating the business environment is being prepared. It aims to reduce the amount of paperwork needed in terms of permits and licences, as well as cutting the activities for which such documents are needed. The plan is to reduce the number of activities for which licensing is needed from 500 to 91, and also to put a halt to regional governments' own licensing procedures (which are already illegal, according to federal law). In addition, a 'one-window' system for company registration is planned. This would eventually mean that when setting up a business there would be only one agency to deal with, instead of the present tortuous procedure of dealing with numerous bureaucrats at various levels, not to mention police and fire departments.

Climate change?

Despite all the cautions and criticism, there is justification for ending this section on a positive note. A survey by the Economist Intelligence Unit, which put questions to 75 large multinational companies operating in Russia, showed that:

- no company in the survey believes that political risk is worsening – 82 per cent feel it is improving and the remainder see no change;

- two-thirds feel that the tax environment is getting better;

- 50 per cent judge Russia as a favourable investment opportunity;

- the majority rate the issue of crime and corruption as manageable or improved;

- more than 60 per cent are operating at pre-crisis levels;

- more than 80 per cent reported making a profit last year;

- more than half expect sales in 2001 to grow between 10 per cent and 25 per cent;

- a quarter expect sales in 2001 to grow between 25 per cent and 50 per cent;

- more than 70 per cent hired new personnel last year and plan to continue hiring in 2001.

Clearly, there have been improvements in the investment climate and in attitudes of investors with a presence in Russia. However, much still needs to be done, and the small size of investments that have reached Russia so far speaks for itself. Also, it often remains hard to convince senior executives of large multinationals that opportunities in Russia can offer high profits.

CAPITAL FLIGHT: THE RUSSIAN MENACE

Capital flight has been a symptom of Russia's failure to establish a functioning market environment. Macroeconomic instability and institutional deficiencies, such as the lack of confidence in the domestic banking system and disincentives to re-invest company profits, have encouraged companies and individuals to move their money offshore. Efforts to combat the problem by introducing capital restrictions have had limited success. A large share of the money moved abroad has left Russia via the trade account by use of false contracts, and by over-reporting imports or under-reporting exports.

Several attempts have been made to quantify the amount of money that has left the country illegally or semi-legally. However, the nature of such flows makes this a difficult task, and reduces estimates to 'guess-timates'. Figure 2.10 presents two alternative measures of capital flight using the balance of payments.

The first estimate (narrow) is made up of non-repatriated export earnings, unredeemed import advances, and errors and omissions. Errors and omissions, which have remained excessively large in the Russian balance of payments, are sometimes referred to as unidentified transfers. The CBR, when estimating capital flight, uses 50 per cent of total errors and omissions. One can use errors and omissions only for

Figure 2.10 *Capital flight*

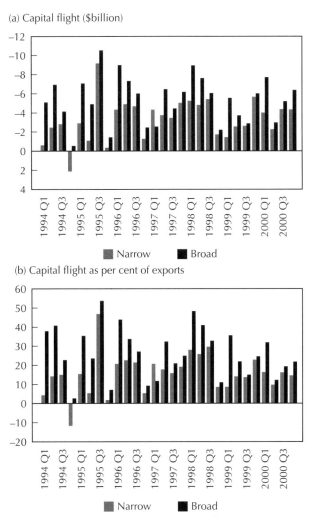

(a) Capital flight ($billion)

(b) Capital flight as per cent of exports

Source: CBR, Goskomstat, own estimates

non-CIS economic relations. However, here the total number of errors and omissions has been included. The second (broad) estimate includes the narrow estimate but also 'overdue payments' on the capital account. The argument here would be that loans are extended by Russian companies to foreign entities, these often being a subsidiary set up by Russian firms, without intention of repayment. These 'loans' are therefore nothing more than a way of moving capital out of Russia.

Estimated capital flight between 1994 and 2000 was close to $100 billion according to the narrow estimate and $155 billion using the broad estimate. This means that on average $1.2 billion or $1.8 billion has left Russia every month during the past seven years, using the narrow and broad estimates respectively. The quarterly pattern shows that in anticipation of a devaluation there was a surge in capital flight in the year before the August 1998 crisis. However, in the following year a clear decline could be observed,[7] explained partly by low world commodity prices and also by short-term effects of the capital restrictions introduced.

Following the OPEC (Organization of Petroleum Exporting Countries) agreement in March 1999 world oil prices rose rapidly, as did natural gas prices with a lag. Furthermore, the constraining effect of capital and foreign exchange restrictions is temporary as economic actors find ways to circumvent them. As a result, the drop in capital flight observed after the crisis was only temporary, and the outflow is now back to levels of $1.5 to $2 billion per month (depending on the estimate). Experts in the Duma, the Russian parliament, announced that capital flight in 2000 amounted to $15 billion. This corresponds exactly with the narrow estimate made here. However, the General Prosecutor's Office quotes a figure between $20 billion and $25 billion.

An interesting development since the crisis has been the possible return of flight capital. Foreign investments into Russia originating from Cyprus and Gibraltar, two countries where much of the flight capital is believed to have ended up, have increased dramatically. In fact, in 1999 these two countries were third and fourth in the foreign investment league, together accounting for 20 per cent of total investments, behind the main investor countries, the US and Germany. And almost half of investments into Russia's metal sector originated from the Antilles. Although these sums are still small, compared with what is flowing out, the fact that Russians are beginning to trust Russia enough to send their money home has to be considered a very positive sign. However, it is much too early to celebrate a turnaround. The only way to create incentives for flight capital to come back to Russia on a large scale is to build a business environment to which capital is ready to return.

CONCLUSION

A central question is: does Russia need foreign investments or do foreign investors need Russia? How much investment Russia needs will depend partly on the pace of economic developments and reforms, especially institutional and structural reforms. Being a major exporter of raw materials and minerals, with world commodity prices remaining high, Russia can grow little and still generate enough revenues to be self-sufficient. Another issue is that of the spill-overs generated by investments, such as know-how and managerial skills. To what extent can these be provided internally? Russia has a highly educated workforce which means that the marginal productivity of human capital should be very high. However, it does not change the fact that the investment climate needs serious improvements, since it is also of decisive importance for domestic investors. Furthermore, a sudden drop in commodity prices would highlight Russia's vulnerability to external factors.

The low levels of foreign investments that Russia has been able to attract so far, and the huge estimates of capital that has left the country, speak for themselves. A healthy investment climate and more investment opportunities are essential to reduce the incentives for capital flight. Opportunities clearly exist, but investors who got their fingers burned by the crisis and by Russia's dubious legal environment will remain cautious. For now, Russia is still an adventure with too many risks.

Notes

[1] Any views and analyses expressed in this chapter should not be assigned to a specific institution to which the author is affiliated.

[2] The figure for Hungary refers to the period 1989–2000, the Czech Republic 1992–2000, and Estonia 1993–2000.

[3] For example La Porta et al., (1998) 'Law and finance', *Journal of Political Economy*, 106 (6), and Levine (1998) 'The legal environment, banks, and long-run economic growth', *Journal of Money, Credit, and Banking*, 30 (3).

[4] La Porta et al., (1997) 'Legal determinants of external finance', *The Journal of Finance*, LII (3), but also La Porta et al., (1998) 'Law and Finance', *Journal of Political Economy*, 106 (6).

[5]Shleifer and Vishny (1997) 'A survey of corporate governance', *The Journal of Finance*, LII (2).

[6] Johnson *et al.,* (1999) 'Contract enforcement in transition', EBRD Working Paper, No. 45.

[7]During the period October 1998 to October 1999 capital flight according to the narrow and broad estimates amounted to $8 billion and $14 billion respectively, an average monthly outflow of $0.7 billion and $1.2 billion.

PART II

Russia: the ultimate adventure

3

TIGHT POLITICS AND EASY ECONOMICS: THE NEW RUSSIAN MODEL AND ITS PARALLEL TO LATIN AMERICA

DEAN LeBARON[1]

M Y FIRST CONTACT WITH THE SOVIET UNION was in 1989 at a meeting in Cambridge, Massachusetts for leaders of the country's military industrial complex to explore how to bring Western capital and Western capitalist practices to enterprises in the Soviet Union. The Soviets sent their first team and the US fielded a class-three farm team. Clearly the Soviets were disappointed and talk among themselves rudely displayed their disinterest in 'not serious' discussions. I was a speaker and seemed to say something that resonated with them. I talked about opportunity to use their world-class technical skills in Western markets. They visited my home – for many, that was the first time they had seen how Westerners, outside of movies, lived their everyday lives. And they came to my office where, at their request, each wanted a one-to-one consultation about their individual problems. Usually these were something along the lines of 'I have 250,000 people employed in my tank factory but only enough work for 5000. Who will fund us until we figure out what else we can do?'

The plan was clear to the Soviets. Reduce military spending on both sides. After all, if there was no cold war threat, why continue to arm against one another? Instead, take part of the hundreds of billions in dollar equivalents and spend it on joint investments. It seemed so simple to them and attractive.

At the invitation of the Gorbachev government, I went to Moscow to see for myself. This visit was arranged within a few days of the invitation since Batterymarch's private plane gave me rather more scheduling flexibility than would normally be possible. I found the problem to be greater than I had imagined. Soviet factories reminded me of scenes from 19th-century English sweatshops. But managers were resourceful in facing problems that would cripple their plants every day and then in solving them. Meanwhile, research facilities, without resources, produced advanced ideas, often without practical application.

I could see that splitting factories into parts would produce smaller units that could be nurtured. Nominally the partnership was between my firm, Batterymarch Financial Management, which was an advisor to major US institutional investors and which had no government affiliation whatsoever, and the Military Industrial Commission (the 'State Commission') whose first deputy chairman, Vladimir Koblov, was our direct liaison. I went to work for about two-and-a-half years with a team of a dozen US and Russian specialists and spent about one week every month in residence. A committee of ministers from the eight ministries that reported to the State Commission was created to guide this joint effort and, most importantly, to learn what we were doing. In the course of our work together, we developed respect for each other and close friendships.

The 5000 military enterprises under the State Commission controlled about 25 per cent of the national economy and certainly its most technologically advanced portion. Otherwise how could it have engendered fear for 50 years in the developed Western economies? Or so the logic went.

Together with Russians from the State Commission, we staffed an office in Moscow across the street from the USA–Canada Institute, a well-regarded think-tank that some said had KGB roots. Our American staff were elegantly housed in a government dacha in Lenin Hills, normally reserved as a guesthouse for official delegations. The residence functioned like the small luxury hotels which have become popular in major cities, although ours might have had special electronics equipment for audio output to receivers in locked rooms in the basement. Russian guests would rarely hold conferences inside, preferring walks in the adjacent and private park grounds.

Although never stated, it was the impression of the Western staff that the privileges we were accorded – access to communications, food from the Kremlin, crack drivers with traffic-stopping rights, and free access in and out of the country in our private plane – indicated that the intelligence services were partners too, and there was a directive by President Mikhail Gorbachev to give us what we needed. We were on a fast track because the Soviets wanted to partner with the West and quickly. They had to get their private economy going because, no matter what, the public economy was imploding.

66 The directors of enterprises were resourceful. Each day they faced new issues which could wipe out their companies. And they survived. 99

Extraordinary people staffed the hundreds of enterprises we saw. With few resources but their own wits, they produced ingenious solutions to problems that we in the West would have solved by buying our way out with more hardware, more factories, more R&D, or more something. These were luxuries not open to the Soviet firms. The directors of enterprises were resourceful. Each day they faced new issues which could wipe out their companies. And they survived. Their systems were dysfunctional but their leaders developed methods to cope. A combination of Western systems and Russian talent would produce dramatic results.

But the odds of finding good enterprises to benefit from new investment were not great. The Soviet companies were huge and cash starved, desperate for cash. This epoch was legendary for its lack of consumer goods and lines waiting for anything. Light bulbs would be taken from fixtures where visitors had been to ones in their new destination. Soap would be put in washrooms just before visitors came and removed very quickly when they left. Food would be hoarded to put on a hospitable spread for guests.

Every enterprise had a conversion programme, trying to find a way to make a living in a non-military, consumer-oriented world. Nobel-prize-class scientists were designing plastic toy pianos for an unknown commercial market. Tank firms talked about car designs and joint ventures.

Now a new effort was made. Politics opened, the press opened, and young reformers were visible in the front ranks of policymakers. The West opened everything except access to enough money, and what came did so to late. Admittedly, more money came through, but it was often in the form of expensive Western infrastructure consulting and not directly to the Soviets. Very little of the give-away – the privatisation – of Russian enterprises went to ordinary people but curiously often benefited a new class of entrepreneurs, the oligarchs, who got very rich on the spoils. The money made in these gray, if not black, markets moved out of Russia in amounts that may have been between $25 billion and $50 billion.

But the West balked at every opportunity to join hands. Perhaps the best effort was the 'Grand Bargain' offered to the Group of 7 industrialized nations (G7) in London in July 1991. President Gorbachev presented a paper jointly authored by Graham Allison, dean of Harvard's Kennedy School, and Grigory Yavlinsky, a highly respected Russian economic reformer. The title, 'Windows of Opportunity: Joint Program for Western Co-operation in the Soviet Transformation to Democracy and the Market Economy', tied specific measures of performance to investment levels. However, attitudes attributed to US President Bush and the Japanese government rejected the idea in its entirety. When this offer became the 'Grand Bust', the Soviet government lost credibility.

A month after the G7 summit, Gorbachev felt his only recourse was to sign an agreement with the Soviet republics known as the Union Treaty. The Soviet central government could no longer impose tax, a power vital to any state, and it was this fiscal impotence that marked the demise of the Soviet Union in December 1991.

The Soviets must also bear some of the blame. Admirable as Gorbachev was, and despite the fact that he was betrayed by the West, he made a fundamental error in trying to reform the political and economic systems simultaneously. Perhaps he was a victim of an aspect of the Russian psyche that was exacerbated under communism – an all-or-nothing extremism.

The West, meanwhile, had 'cheaped out'. I believe that a straight line led from the G7 meeting to the Union Treaty and, in August 1991, to tanks on the streets of Moscow.

With a group of investors, I arrived in Moscow on Sunday night, 18 August, 1991, the eve of the kidnapping of Gorbachev and his wife and the launch of a coup attempt by a group of hardliners. On 22 August, 1991, the third day of the attempted coup, we met in Leningrad with the city's mayor, Anatoly Sobchak, and other anti-coup stalwarts who had congregated to defend the government offices there. One of Mayor Sobchak's key aides at the meeting was Vladimir Putin, who eight years later would become president. Having served as a colonel with the KGB in East Germany, Putin had moved to Leningrad and the offices of Mayor Sobchak, his former professor, where he was put in charge of the city's privatisation and sale of state assets. (By December, the city was again called St Petersburg, its original name.)

If the first phase of the political/economic transformation was Gorbachev's attempt to consumerize the Soviet economy within the structure of the Soviet Union, the second started in August 1991, with the failed coup attempt and the ultimate dissolution of the Soviet Union in December 1991. After the failed coup, the Soviet Union entered its brief twilight. Gorbachev returned to the presidency of a country that was falling apart around him. The real power shifted to Boris Yeltsin, the president of the now independant Russia. Yeltsin was given the mandate. And just as the West had done, Yeltsin also humiliated Mikhail Gorbachev.

My mandate came from the Soviet government, specifically its president, Mikhail Gorbachev. So when the August 1991 coup took place, the message was clear: a new government team would take over. Six months later we packed up and left.

Despite the command economy's faults, some aspects of it could have proven useful in the transition period. In fact, some were essential in the same way that strong leadership is essential to any company that is re-engineering from old processes to new. It is difficult to be democratic when the job is to allocate scarce resources for future development rather than to satisfy immediate needs. The weakening of central authority damaged the reform process.

A period of confusion, looting of assets, and emergence of an openly expressive society became evident in the next eight years. Gross domestic product, as best one can determine from figures, declined steadily. The term 'bandit capitalism' seemed to fit. Economics were modelled more after that on the docks of Hoboken, New Jersey than on mid-American free enterprise. Security meant paying for protection. And still no one tried to do anything for the people on the street, who would stay on the street. We know the result of the bandit capitalism. It is estimated that hundreds of billions of dollars worth of state assets have moved into a few private hands, with the acquiescence of Western officials.

Observers of Russia see crime as endangering both the country's fragile democracy and its newly born free market. Yet, paradoxically, the various 'mafiyas' enjoyed a modicum of respect among the citizenry because they were able to impose and maintain a semblance of order.

It may be incorrect to view the government and the mafiyas as two distinct entities. Russian politics always had a criminal aspect – tsardom was once defined as absolute tyranny tempered by assassination – and Stalin was certainly a criminal by any legal standard. In the 1990s, neither the people in the government, who had something to hide, nor the mafiyas wanted a stable political climate. Steady, reliable governments will not tolerate this level of corruption and criminality. An unbalanced power structure means political instability, the enemy of genuine prosperity.

For Russia, capital flight has been a dominant feature of the past decade, perhaps in the tens of billions of dollars each year. One can assume that almost none of it was entirely legally obtained – money laundering, false accounting statements, and tax evasion are rarely prosecuted as crimes in the Russian systems. Curiously the present atmosphere of stability seems accompanied by a continuation of money outflow, perhaps even an increase. But foreign investments are a counterbalancing inflow.

The Russian public, normally passive and tolerant, and especially the free press, could not reconcile the bandit capitalism – and the speeding private limousines, the bodyguards in chase vehicles, the contract killings – with the poverty on the streets. After nearly a decade of free politics and free economics, this second phase of Russian transformation was over. A quest for a strong hand and pride in one's country set the stage for a turn to General Pinochet … excuse me, I mean Colonel Putin.

We have just entered a new phase, one without origin on Russian soil. Now there is an elected government, rumoured to have been selected by some of the oligarchs, which appears determined to reinstate pride in central control. The young reformers are still present with their economic plans, but press criticism of the government has been curbed. The military has been offered more support. And the oligarchs who may have helped select President Vladimir Putin (who may have been a member of that same oligarch circle) may get a little slap on the wrist. In other words, the new scheme will run the country on tight politics and easy economics.

A military takeover in Russia remained, for a time, a strong possibility. The army, the one institution that always functioned well in the Soviet Union, retained some of its traditional prestige. There seems to be little doubt that Putin was placed in the offices of prime minister and later as president to forestall something that would be worse for the 'family' – a military coup that was not of their initiation. His charge might have been, like Pinochet's in Chile, to restore national pride and leave the economy free to function on global rules under the direction of the leading business forces already in place.

While Russia plunges towards an autocratic, single-theme model – restore pride in the central state – Western governments look for active dissent as a sign that democratic leanings have not been stifled. It would be consistent with the multi-strategy Russian mind to provide evidence of some dissent but in a carefully controlled manner. So it is possible to detect the move of a seemingly non-government party under the direction of Boris Berezovsky, who might be principally responsible for appointing Putin to the leadership in the first place.

Thus, evidence of dissent could be found but orchestrated behind the scenes. And real dissent in the form of press freedoms would continue to be curbed.

It may be that Putin will compromise with a blend of capitalism, social freedom and authoritarian rule. Under Putin, Russia is more likely to have a nationalist party that monopolizes power rather than a reversion to communism. Having broken its ties with communism, Russia will, most likely, include some communist rhetoric and policies in its nationalist programme but will base its legitimacy on other foundations.

If it sounds like Chile under General Pinochet, it is. Exactly. General Pinochet was selected, it is rumoured, by the oligarchs of Chile to correct the communist policies of his predecessor. They wanted secure politics and freedom to develop markets without government interference. One of the first sectors they chose to develop was the management of private savings by, not surprisingly, private financial firms, the very ones which supported Pinochet. And Chile was the better for it. The country knew where it was going. It was not just a level playing field, it was a carefully mapped one.

My experience in Chile began in the late 1980s following the founding by my firm, in 1987, of the first institutional equity fund to invest in Brazil. In one of the first meetings with officials in Santiago, I visited the Finance Ministry for lunch. A group of senior, grey-suited officials hosted an early afternoon meeting covering the usual topics of monetary export controls, currency conversions, market restrictions for foreigners and the like. Any of the participants could have been the finance minister, whom I did not expect to be present. Shortly, a California 'beachboy-like' person arrived wearing, I noticed, open sandals. He sat on the floor. I thought he could have been a translator, but I guessed wrong. This was Hernan Buchci, the reform-minded finance minister. Free market reform combined with cattle-prod politics was the rule.

66 Under Putin, Russia is more likely to have a nationalist party that monopolizes power rather than a reversion to communism. 99

Of course Chile is not the only recent historical case blending tight politics and easy economics. South Korea, Singapore, Malaysia and

Taiwan come to mind, among others. In each situation there was a ruling élite in a position to exploit the climate of privatisation for themselves in close partnership with government. And the economies flourished. It is a model of some success and even parallels the practice of Russia's new partner, China. (Leaders of the Soviet Union once derided the Chinese to me as 'our little yellow communist cousins'. They now mimic and respect the Chinese.)

Today, looking at Putin's Russia, I think of Pinochet's Chile. If the parallel holds, the prospect for the future, economically at least, is quite attractive. Chile has been a model for investment success in Latin America since that time.

Note

[1]Any views and analyses expressed in this chapter should not be assigned to a specific institution to which the author is affiliated.

4

RUSSIAN CAPITAL MARKETS 1994–2001: A GROUND-LEVEL ACCOUNT

PETER M. HALLORAN

M Y VENTURE INTO THE FLEDGLING CAPITAL MARKETS of Russia began in January 1994 as simply a great trade opportunity. At that time, few Westerners were even aware that the market for Russian privatisation vouchers existed. Meanwhile, CS First Boston had exiled some newly minted bankers to its Moscow office to give free advice on privatisation to the government. The real opportunity, however, turned out to be organizing the local brokers to source for Western clients – I provided the clients from New York, the Moscow office organized the brokers. The success of this early voucher activity became the launching point for all that followed.

THE VOUCHER ADVENTURE

The mathematics of the voucher privatisation trade was quite simple. Every citizen was issued a free voucher as their birthright, totalling roughly 148 million. These vouchers traded in the range of $12–$18 each, thus valuing a large foothold in the asset base of Russia at between $1.8 billion and $2.7 billion. I remember 'research' that we put together for voucher auctions. The meagre entries typically included such illuminating facts as company name, company address, number of employees, percentage of shares to be auctioned and industry category. But with dreams of untold resource riches, not to mention some industrial assets, little additional analysis was needed.

The voucher auctions became a battle of information and misinformation. Often managements looking to buy their own shares would hold the auction in an obscure location with minimal notice. For the larger enterprises, the game among investors was to guess how many vouchers might be bid by others in order to avoid pushing the price too high. A great coup was being able to find an overlooked company where only a few vouchers could buy an entire auction. Thus investors were always careful to keep their true interests as quiet as possible.

Most of the activity took place over a short period in the spring of 1994. The last significant enterprise to be auctioned was Norilsk Nickel on 30 June, 1994, for which almost all remaining vouchers were used. Thus the now famous Russian voucher activity actually took place over just a few frenetic months. It was the immediate post-voucher period that became even more frenzied as the summer of 1994 saw dollar flows continue even though vouchers had expired and very few companies were yet eligible to trade. The result was a bubble that lasted until Mexico's peso was devalued later that year.

A greater mania in the region took place in Azerbaijan in 1998, fuelled largely by those who had missed out on Russian privatisation. Again, free vouchers had been issued to all citizens, but few enterprises were ever made available for auction. The key asset that drove the market valuation of Azeri vouchers was the state oil company, SOCAR. Unlike with Russia, Westerners began buying Azeri vouchers much before plans for the privatisation of SOCAR had been announced. As a result, the mathematics of the trade was much murkier. Without SOCAR there was very little worth buying with vouchers in Azerbaijan. The market price of a voucher settled around an assumption that 5 per cent of SOCAR would be offered through the voucher mechanism, a mechanism from which the state received no proceeds. The Azeri mania began in earnest when an alternate assumption was introduced to the market by a self-interested broker that fully 50 per cent of SOCAR would be handed out for free through a voucher auction. The vouchers, according to this assumption, were thus undervalued tenfold. The Westerners caught up in the mania failed to notice that the same broker was selling them his own position. In the end, none of SOCAR was privatized, meaning the Azeri vouchers were actually overvalued tenfold. This example shows that, by comparison, Russia has done some things correctly along the way.

Such voucher mania never fully reached Ukraine. While a similar voucher system was devised, few meaningful enterprises came available. As a result, the Ukrainian stock market consisted mainly of blocs of shares being horse traded in sizes designed to create either blocking minority stakes (25 per cent plus one share) or controlling majority stakes (50 per cent plus one share). With Russia having already drawn investors to the region, there was clearly an opportunity for Ukraine as these same investors began hunting for comparable opportunities in nearby Kiev. The deputy prime minister in 1996, Viktor Pynznyk, recognized the opportunity. On a random trip to Kiev, I met Pynznyk on behalf of CSFB and he offered to sell controlling stakes in two of the four major electricity utilities. We discussed how this transaction was exactly what Ukraine needed to create liquidity and jump-start its equity market.

The idea was to sell the shares on to portfolio investors in the West. I bid him that day in excess of $100 million, an amount that was quite reasonable for us both at the time. He promised to get back to me after consulting with his boss, Prime Minister Pavel Lazarenko. Unfortunately, he never called back. Instead, our Kiev office called to say Pynznyk had abruptly resigned from the government – Ukraine had thus indicated its true interest in privatisation. While I cannot confirm the motives for cancelling the privatisation, I can confirm that the former prime minister, Lazarenko, is in custody facing charges for enriching himself while in office.

THE ERA OF THE OLIGARCHS

Russia had its own unique version of such a large-scale transfer of assets for cash. But unlike with Pynznyk, the motivations were not quite honourable. This was the 'loans-for-shares' scheme. Originally voucher privatisation was intended to create a market into which cash privatisations could be sold. The state was to raise revenues during this second stage. It never happened.

Instead moneyed insiders hatched an idea in early 1995 to co-opt the process. At the time the Russian equity market was struggling. In addition, state coffers were low due to inept fiscal planning and an inability to collect taxes. The idea was simple – banks would lend money to the state in return for holding controlling stakes in some of Russia's largest enterprises as collateral. Once control was taken, the cash flows of the enterprises were diverted through banks owned by the oligarchs. With a payment system that included barter, there were endless opportunities to make money in such a scheme.

The loans came due a year later as the equity market was booming. Not surprisingly, however, the government allowed the oligarchs to effectively foreclose on the loans by allowing them to be sold through rigged auctions organized by the oligarchs themselves. Often the purchase price barely exceeded the windfall already received by the oligarchs simply from having controlled the enterprise for a year. Even more perversely, the original loans themselves were often simply government funds on deposit with an oligarch acting as clearing agent for the Ministry of Finance. Thus the oligarchs never needed cash, just connections.

One deal that had not been earmarked for such abuse was the sale of an 8.5 per cent stake of Unified Energy Systems, which was to be auctioned for a minimum of $325 million in 1997. In November 1996, CSFB announced that it would organize the auction in the form of convertible bonds to be issued the following year. As the market had cooled considerably, the prevailing logic was that an auction should wait for conditions to improve. Also the management were likely to be replaced in the spring, and with an improvement in market sentiment, the sale could likely fetch a better price by waiting. These visions of a better auction environment were overwhelmed by realism which made it apparent that waiting could be even more dangerous as assets seemed to be disappearing from the auction block.

"the oligarchs never needed cash, just connections"

It was already November 1996 and Alfred Kokh, the privatisation minister, was under pressure as the loans-for-shares giveaways had left him short of his 1996 revenue targets. If Kokh could be persuaded to launch an early sale, I knew of a deep-pocketed investor who could quickly commit to the entire purchase. When both parties had agreed, the remaining problem became time. According to Russian law the auction would need to stay open for 30 days, but if the revenues hit before the end of January 1997, Kokh could credit them to his 1996 budget.

Kokh shocked the market when he announced the auction with a bid deadline of 20 December. At first it was dismissed as year-end posturing; few believed there could be a buyer for such size. The minimum price for the auction was set 20 per cent above the market at 9.2 cents per share – $325 million, all or none.

As the market came to understand that CSFB did have a buyer, the Duma quickly responded with a vote of 270–0 to cancel the auction to prevent a sale to foreigners. But, even worse, Gazprom, Russia's gas monopoly, decided it wanted the stake itself. Those were the days of massive payment arrears, and UES was a sizeable debtor to its fuel supplier Gazprom. As the endgame was played, National Reserve Bank (NRB), a Gazprom-linked entity, emerged as another buyer. It was difficult to imagine it had $325 million cash to spend on UES shares, but it pushed forward as the only other bidder.

The auction procedure required a refundable deposit of the full bid amount to be deposited several days before the bids were due. We decided to deposit a much larger amount than we actually intended to bid, in hopes of dissuading the other bidder. While the process was supposed to be blind, we learned after the deposit deadline that NRB had placed some very small amount just in excess of our deposit amount. The next step in the 'blind' process was the bid itself. At this point we bid the minimum on the assumption that the outcome depended only on whether the other bidder was real, not the amount we might choose to bid. True to our expectations, NRB won the auction by bidding exactly one rouble per share above us. Brilliant insight on their part? The saddest part of the tale appears to be that no actual cash made its way to the budget; instead budgetary offsets were allowed to create cash value. This experience confirmed that the state at that time was not being managed in the interest of maximizing revenues.

The most infamous cash auction of all was the privatisation of Svyazinvest, the state telecom holding company. With a 51 per cent stake in nearly every incumbent provider in Russia, it represented huge untapped opportunity. Western investors were invited to participate for the first time given the high asking price of $1.1 billion. At that time telecoms globally were starting to be re-rated by investors who saw them as an all-important link to the consumer. Svyazinvest had access to 148 million consumers – and it was for sale.

As the last of the big cash auctions, the eventual winner decided as a combination of oligarchs, including Mikhail Friedman of Alfa Bank and Vladimir Gusinsky of Media-Most. As the asking price was $1.1 billion, an amount the oligarchs were unwilling to stake themselves, Alfa was appointed to source the funds from Western investors. For this it turned to CSFB, and I started the process before leaving for the Christmas break in 1996. At that time, as with the UES auction, there was little demand for Russian shares that were already up 123 per cent for the year.

Nonetheless, there were some large, non-traditional buyers who had shown interest in Russia. They were very quick to embrace the idea of effectively financing the oligarch's acquisition of Svyazinvest, and upon arriving back in New York for Christmas the money had been raised. Alfa Bank was puzzled, and decided that perhaps its terms had been too generous. It chose not to accept the financing consortium and instead turned to a competitor for help – on worse terms. After a couple of months had passed without result, Alfa returned to accept our financial consortium.

It had waited too long. By this time the stock market was booming again and the regional telecoms underlying Svyazinvest were the leading gainers. Svyazinvest had also caught the attention of the other oligarchs. They understood that the last jewel was about to be sold, and decided to break with the original plan and participate in the auction. Thus began the first real cash auction in Russia.

The implications of this were numerous, and mostly negative. The CSFB-financed consortium ultimately had the deepest pockets, which included a strategic partner, yet lost the bid. It remains a subject of heated debate whether it was simply poor bidding strategy or otherwise. The resultant hard feelings continue to be played out today as Gusinsky faces many of the same adversaries in his struggle for NTV as he did with the Svyazinvest auction.

Svyazinvest became the catalyst for driving apart the fragile alignment of oligarchs in Russia. The result was a series of open disputes that ultimately tainted the legitimacy of the government. The timing was disastrous, as the government was just about to launch reforms under its 'dream team' of Boris Nemstov and Anatoly Chubais. With a leaderless state under Yeltsin, and the oligarchs going their separate ways, there was little that the dream team could hope to accomplish. Their downfall released a series of events culminating in the debt default of 1998.

THE CRISIS: CRIME AND PUNISHMENT

The August 1998 devaluation, default and moratorium were a shock to the global markets. The devaluation itself was less of a shock, and already priced into the markets. Many fixed-income investors had already arranged the duration of their portfolios sufficiently to weather a 50 per cent devaluation near term, yet have adequate dollar returns on their longer-dated paper. But the default was the unexpected event. And the moratorium was the criminal act.

The moratorium confirmed the statelessness of Russia under Yeltsin. Here was a nation exercising its sovereign authority not to protect its own interests but rather those of a chosen élite. Quite simply, the moratorium was designed to protect the oligarchs. The moratorium gave enough time to shift title to assets while leaving behind billions in liabilities, mainly to Westerners and Russia's emerging middle class.

The Westerners' GKO adventure had really begun in earnest in early 1996. At that time the Russian government had embarked upon an expensive pre-election spending spree. As the country was awash in wage and pension arrears from the government, Yeltsin was in need of cash in a hurry to win over the masses. To do this, the T-bill market,

GKOs, was expanded from $8 billion outstanding to what would become an eightfold increase over two years. Pre-election yields quickly tripled from 50 per cent to more than 150 per cent during the weekly auctions.

Officially, non-residents were not allowed to participate. Yet, to be successful, the government needed to tap into Western flows. In fact, at CSFB we often had sufficient demand to buy the entire weekly auction. They were willing to let us in on an ad hoc basis, always with special Central Bank approvals designed to emphasize the temporary nature of the situation. Eventually the Ministry of Finance understood the inevitability of their needs and created a non-resident investment mechanism called an 'S-account'. All dollar flows from the West destined for the GKO market, and hopefully back, had to pass through this S-account window.

The idea was that the window could be opened or closed as needed, and all GKO flows could be closely monitored. It was intended as a clever way of controlling the flows, and as importantly, controlling the growing monopoly we had at CSFB of bringing investors into the market. Instead, the unintended result was that the S-account became a mechanism for more Western banks to set up their own proprietary accounts to control the client flows they brought into Russia.

By 1997 the short-term GKOs were on the way to being replaced by more stable dollar financing through the eurobond market. This transition was well under way at the end of 1997 when a global liquidity crisis foreclosed that opportunity. Instead, Russia found itself faced with a classic short-term funding squeeze – a squeeze the IMF was set up to prevent. The problem continued as it became apparent that no amount of money could offset the oligarchs' lack of confidence in the rouble. They feared their hard-won gains could not survive the growing intervention of the West. This fear, coupled with the relative inexperience of the oligarchs and government ministers with financial markets, caused them to panic together in August, forcing a sweeping cancellation of obligations. It was not altogether different than when children ask for a do-over when things do not go their way on the playground.

WINDS OF CHANGE?

The question most asked today is whether investors will return to Russia. The answer, if framed only in the context of the debt default, appears to be yes. Let me give an example. In June 2000 17 per cent of Moscow mobile provider MTS was sold in an initial public offering (IPO) for over $300 million. The sad history behind that offering is that a roughly equal amount of shares of MTS had been stripped from the city wire line incumbent, MGTS, by its controlling shareholder. The minority shareholders of MGTS at the time received almost nothing for the stake that was essentially being sold back to many of these same investors for $300 million.

It is more appropriate to frame questions regarding the return of Western shareholders in the context of the pace of Russia's transition. Expectations today are both more informed and reluctant. To combine vast natural resources and a well-educated people with an entirely new social and economic system is really not so easy. The real question being asked by investors is about the realistic timetable for change. Although reforms have been proposed repeatedly since 1996, the pace of their implementation has been the key disappointment. To date Vladimir Putin has implemented more reform than during Yeltsin's final term. That is at least encouraging.

66 The question most asked today is whether investors will return to Russia. 99

In many ways the dilemma for Russia is the same as that seen in other resource-rich countries. How can oil-rich Nigeria founder while resource-poor Japan becomes an economic power? It is sometimes true that an abundance of easy wealth prevents the proper organization of a society – a bit like a 'trust fund kid' lacking the proper motivations to improve himself. To succeed in an era of global capitalism, Russia must learn to recognize the concept of property. Otherwise the willing exchange of risk between parties cannot develop and, without such an exchange of risk, free markets do not function.

At present there are no competing ideologies to that of global capitalism. The rewards to participating are so apparent that even North Korea is asking to be included. So the question is not whether but how Russia will participate in global capitalism. The restructuring of Unified Energy Systems serves as a useful example. While all parties agree that the restructuring should be market oriented, none is willing to cede access or control to achieve this end. As a result, the implementation of changes already agreed for UES has become mired in skirmishes for control. And so has Russia.

5

THE RUSSIAN CRISIS: WHAT THE RUSSIA ANALYSTS 'MISSED', 1990–8

LETITIA RYDJESKI[1]

I WORKED AS AN ANALYST COVERING East Central Europe and Russia from 1990, before the Soviet Union collapsed, to just before the August 1998 default. During this time, the emerging market world experienced two major shocks – that of Mexico in December 1994 and Asia in late 1997 early 1998. In both the Mexican and Asian cases, emerging markets analysts did not predict the crises. The main lesson the emerging markets community learned from Mexico was that a large current account deficit cannot be financed by speculative, short-term capital. From Asia, the emerging markets community learned that very high levels of internal debt are not sustainable, and pegged currencies in relatively open market economies can collapse from the weight of this debt. On both occasions the crises seemingly appeared out of nowhere, and took the market by surprise. Similarly, while it was obvious that the Russian local debt market was in deep trouble by the spring of 1998, analysts did not foresee the Russian debt default, and only a few suspected that the Russian GKO market would collapse even weeks before it actually did. The Russian market crashed because the government had relied too heavily on speculative, short-term capital to finance its fiscal deficit. Could some rough parallels not have been drawn between Russia and the Mexico crisis?

After the Russian crash, one of the major issues in my mind as a (former) analyst was just what the emerging market analyst community had failed to see about Russia, and why analysts couldn't predict market stress in view of the fact that emerging markets had gone through two major crises already. What were the symptoms of the crisis and why did we not (choose to) see them?

Most of the financial community (along with the US and Western European governments) deluded itself about Russia during the 1990s. There was too much faith that Russia would pull itself through its problems, and that the overwhelming transition in the economy and political system would occur without major hitches. However, during the years leading up to the default and devaluation, there were numerous signs that the Russian market was becoming progressively compromised, and the financial community failed to understand or ignored these signs. Here we will provide a non-rigorous examination of pre-crisis indications – some of them of an unconventional nature – that the Russian market was headed for trouble, as seen by an 'outside' analyst at the time.

TRADITIONAL MACROECONOMIC MEASURES

There is arguably little point in dissecting macroeconomic indicators in discussing the reasons for Russia's crash. Most economic statistics were indicative at best, and none of them could have ultimately predicted the crash itself. Moreover, typical Western macroeconomic measures were inapplicable to much of the post-Soviet economy anyway, as almost all of the economy basically still functioned much like its Soviet predecessor, and we had no way of determining whether economic activity as described in 'Soviet' terms had been converted, so to speak, to traditional Western economic terms. For example, during the 1990s, monetization of the economy was very low, and a lot of economic transactions used barter, mutual debt cancellations, or the 'wechsel' (promissory note) system. To what extent was such economic activity captured by traditional Western economic measures? How could we reconcile the fact that industrial production had collapsed with the fact that electricity use by industry did not register equivalent falls?

As for those indicators that analysts did try to monitor closely, the current account typically registered on paper a sizeable surplus due to capital flight, which contributed to the crash. The current account could have been a rough indicator, as it gave some indication of the enormous sums of hard currency leaving the country, thus theoretically making the Russian market vulnerable to a currency crisis. The rouble exchange band was unsustainable in the long term, and survived as long as it did only thanks to significant IMF support. This aspect was often shunted to the background, so that the currency was actually more vulnerable than people realized or acknowledged. However, while the genesis of the crisis could be found in traditional economic measures, such as capital flight and the lack of fiscal and structural reform, the final reasons and timing of the crash were largely political, as the analyst community could have foreseen if it had known Russia, and particularly the Soviet Union, better. Such better knowledge would have involved less attention to the traditional macroeconomic factors and more to atypical issues such as politics and corruption.

LACK OF KNOWLEDGE OF THE SOVIET UNION

Arguably the most important reason for the analyst community failing to see the makings of the Russian crash was that most analysts did not understand the essence of the Soviet system. A lot of the indications that the Russian market was compromised by the mid-1990s were due to the fact that many aspects of the old Soviet system were intact, and they would ultimately bring down the reform attempt (or pseudo-reform attempt). The personalization of power, the constitution that heavily favoured the presidency, the rise of an oligarchy, the lack of a civil code and civil society, the failure of structural reform, the lack of domestic investment, and most importantly, the overall corruption of society all had their roots in the Soviet system, and ultimately symbolized the glaring lack of reform. Analysts who visited Russia during these years had a variety of knowledge of the Soviet system, but few if any had much experience in the Soviet system itself.

Analysts are always cautioned against becoming journalists or historians in their written work, and told that they must concentrate on the future versus the past in their analysis. This is certainly a valid approach. However, Russia is a market where the historical, economic and political legacy is so enormous that analysts should have been cautioning more about the precarious future of reform due to the unparalleled economic distortions caused by the Soviet past. Russia had arguably the smallest presence of any real market in the economy of any emerging market country (even parts of Eastern Europe had remnants of a market economy – or at least some collective memory of a market economy – in the years leading up to transformation). Moreover, there was no history of civil society or civil law in Russia. There was an awareness of this shortcoming in the analyst community, but certainly little appreciation of the scale of problems that it could cause. Thus, in the end, if the analyst community had concentrated more on history, perhaps we would have realized that the changeover to a liberal market economy would be a very long-term process (50 years or more) and that Russia would never adopt Western ways in the short term – and may not even adopt them in the long term.

66 **there was no history of civil society or civil law in Russia** 99

THE NOMENKLATURA SYSTEM AND ITS CONTINUED STRENGTH

Probably most analysts knew something of the Soviet nomenklatura system, which in the former Soviet Union gave the Communist Party élite control over information, resources and decision making. Certainly fewer analysts had an accurate idea of just how pervasive and resourceful this system was. When the government of Yegor Gaidar made its well-intentioned but blundering reform efforts in 1991–3, well-placed industrial directors, including those in the all-important energy sector, and to some extent banking leaders (a lot of them former members of the Soviet nomenklatura), were able to position themselves auspiciously and obstruct any further reform efforts in their enterprises and industrial sectors. Central government control by the reformists was very weak in the early 1990s. Thus the new (and old) Russian nomenklatura took its chance to seize control of state assets, largely before most Western 'outside' analysts were able to determine the direction of the reform effort, much less grasp the lasting influence of the Soviet nomenklatura system.

During 1991–3, when the only legitimate attempts at reform were made, two forces, the reformers and the self-aggrandisers (a name given to the entire spectrum of those who illegitimately benefited from the reforms, from the richest oligarchs to small enterprise directors), began their struggle for influence. Self-aggrandisers were politically well represented in parliament, and were politically very well prepared for taking on the weak, disorganized Gaidar government. The fight for control over resources and its huge importance to the success or failure of the reform attempt was not obvious in Russian analysis in the early years, even though this control had been one of the main pillars of Soviet strength, both economic and political. The analyst community apparently failed to draw the parallel with how, in Soviet times, a tight hold on resources, from oil to minerals to infrastructure, plus control of information ensured power for the Communists. After the Communist state had disintegrated, the same hold over resources would again ensure power, both economic and political, to the winners in the new system. The fight for control of resources gained real attention only after 1993, when the future oligarchy was beginning to take shape via concentration of control over major sectors of the economy in fewer and fewer hands.

LIMITING OURSELVES TO PRO-WESTERN MOSCOVITE OR ST PETERSBURG LIBERALS

Visits to Moscow by outside analysts concentrated on meetings with the reformist elements in Russia. Meetings typically concentrated on the IMF or World Bank representatives, Central Bank officials, and more liberal individuals in government, banking and political circles. Meetings in the early years with anyone truly outside liberal, pro-Western circles were a rarity. Those meetings that did occur were more often of the 'side-show' variety, such as press conferences given by Liberal-Democratic Party leader Vladimir Zhirinovsky or Communist Party leader Gennady Zyuganov. For those who spoke Russian, it was easy enough to get appointments with people who were not in the newspapers, and who had little to lose by saying how things really were. Often these were journalists or mid-level academics in research institutes who observed the political scene and could relate it to the Soviet system. They were able to combine the Soviet past with the progress of Russian reform for an accurate analysis. As they were not particularly prominent, their views did not make the analyst reports. And, as a lot of outside analysts did not speak fluent Russian, they were not able to access these people very easily.

Moreover, with the exception of equity analysts, few analysts ever ventured out of Moscow or St Petersburg. Certainly few, if any, sovereign analysts ever ventured beyond the two largest cities, which were very unrepresentative of the rest of the country. While most relevant information for analysts was indeed obtainable only in Moscow or St Petersburg, ignoring how the rest of Russia lived or thought was also a mistake. The cost and time-effectiveness of provincial trips is certainly debatable, but the end effect of geographic limitation was simply a lack of knowledge about Russia. By concentrating on the liberal, pro-Western elements in Moscow and St Petersburg, the analysts ended up aligning themselves with the weaker elements in the medium-term struggle for reform and failing to acquaint themselves with the stronger elements. (By way of example of how the 'rest of Russia' differed from Moscow and St Petersburg, Vladimir Zhirinovsky and his Liberal-Democratic Party's strong showing in the December 1993 parliamentary elections came as a surprise to the West. Unscientific opinion polls conducted by myself through individuals in selected areas outside Moscow and St Petersburg in the lead-up to the elections showed Zhirinovsky with an undeniable lead in these provincial areas. However, as these polls were so unscientific and geographically diffuse, their results could not be regarded as accurate and were never promulgated. In hindsight, however, the polls provided a valuable lesson: Moscow was very unrepresentative of Russia as a whole.)

'OUR MAN CHUBAIS' AND LOANS-FOR-SHARES

Just as the US government aligned itself too much with President Boris Yeltsin and failed to make inroads into finding potential allies elsewhere, the Western financial world pinned too many hopes on Anatoly Chubais. In the early years there was much more reason to support Chubais, as he was clearly one of the leaders of the liberal, pro-Western reform effort. However, after his misguided 'loans-for-shares' programme in 1995, the outside analyst community should have questioned his economic and political judgement more than it did. Chubais may well have faced a Faustian choice of selling off some of the choicest state assets at cut-rate prices to gain the oligarchs' support in face of a potential Communist threat in the 1996 presidential elections. The oligarchs' financial and political support for Yeltsin's presidential campaign was undeniably vital. However, loans-for-shares was probably the all-corrupting point of no return in the entire reform effort.

The reality of the loans-for-shares programme became evident right off when the programme was launched in late 1995, and with this the Russian market was irreversibly compromised. The analyst community quickly became aware of the rigged auction procedures, the predetermined distribution of assets among cronies and potential economic and political patrons, but there was little outcry over the corruption of the entire affair. The presence of the oligarchy was already obvious, and the division of economic spoils was being fought out in public prior to the loans-for-shares programme. In explaining the corruption at the time, there were some weak parallels drawn between the Russian oligarchs of the late 20th century and the American robber-barons of the 19th century. However, even a cursory study of the American robber-barons will show that, in contrast to the Russian oligarchs, they created value and wealth even in the short term, despite their questionable and sometimes repugnant methods. Russian oligarchs were simply swiping assets for their own self-aggrandisement. There was no real value or wealth created, and long-term wealth effects are doubtful. Loans-for-shares demonstrated the destructiveness of the self-aggrandisers and their pernicious effects on the entire community, an unfortunate fact that was never fully appreciated or acknowledged by the outside world, the analyst community included, until it was too late.

THE 'BANKING' SYSTEM

The banking system hardly deserved the name. Several thousand different institutions, most of them far too small and undercapitalized to be considered banks, existed on subsidised government credits and developed with time into foreign exchange speculators and GKO (treasury bond) flipping houses. Even the large banks hardly carried on any true banking activity. There was no real commercial lending as there was no investment in the real economy for which to provide loans. Before the GKO heyday it was hard at first glance to figure out just how the banks survived. Questions put to banking officials were not met with straight answers. Those banks with government connections were able to hold budget funds and use them for various speculative activities, mostly currency speculation. Once the treasury market picked up in 1995 the banks used the government's dire need to raise funds, and the yields it was willing to pay, to keep themselves afloat.

The few thousand smaller banks that analysts tended to ignore were a strong symptom of the system's problems. A few people with some cash and good connections could establish a bank, but the bank's only purpose was to promote the owner's wealth. Such a parasitic function of so-called banks was a huge weight on the economy, a fact not truly appreciated by the analyst community. The same parasitic aspect was even truer for the larger, oligarch-owned banks. These banks merely existed as money-collection and distribution centres for the particular oligarch's financial and economic interests. When a few of these banks issued eurobonds in the mid-1990s, there were even attempts at serious analysis of these banks as actual banks, which now appear as examples of extreme economic denial.

TOO BIG TO FAIL

Mostly uttered in 1998, after the Asian crisis had ravaged emerging markets and the investor community was beginning to face the truth about Russia's precarious state, the words 'too big to fail' connected Russia's fate with the IMF. Presumably the IMF would not let Russia crash, as the effects would overwhelm already battered emerging markets. Even up to a few weeks before the August 1998 crash these words were being used to argue that Russia would avoid the same fate as some of the Asian markets. Ultimately, however, neither the IMF nor any other international effort could have saved Russia. There were insufficient resources to 'save' the country and by the summer of 1998 it was obvious that Russia's use of IMF funds was suspicious to say the least. The 'too big to fail' argument was another example of the Russia delusion that the outside world experienced during the 1990s.

THE HUNT FOR YIELD IN 1996–7

Many emerging market yields had fallen significantly during the two years before the Asian crisis in late 1997. A number of emerging market countries had seen credit upgrades, thus their bond yield spreads had shrunk. Greater demand for emerging market fixed-income assets had also pushed down yields, especially in emerging Europe, where supply was quite limited to begin with. By 1996 emerging market asset managers were hunting for yield and Russia became still more attractive as it provided comparatively high yields. Squeezed by the credit-ratings 'inflation' that was particularly evident in Asia, asset managers were too eager to buy into higher-yielding Russian debt to enhance portfolio returns. The most extreme example of this was Russia's GKO (local treasury) market. In the midst of the environment of ratings inflation, the perception of Russian risk also diminished. At the time the Russian market appeared almost charmed as its risk appeared to be lowering while it still offered relatively high yields.

> **The GKO frenzy was the epitome of the hunt for yield and the investor onslaught in the Russian market**

The GKO frenzy was the epitome of the hunt for yield and the investor onslaught in the Russian market. Correspondingly, GKOs were bound to be the focal point of the crash. The volumes at which the government was issuing GKOs and the tremendous yields that the government was willing to pay investors should have been a warning sign long before the actual crash. It should have been obvious that the government was way over its head in debt, and was issuing new debt mostly to repay old debt. The lack of fiscal reform through the years should also have been a major warning sign that the GKO system was likely to be dragged under at some point. When the GKO market experienced a yield scare early in 1998, it did give the investor community some pause. There was an unspoken realization among some in the market that the government was indebted beyond its means to repay. However, the 'too big to fail' mentality started to take hold in the spring of 1998.

Once Asia had experienced its crash in late 1997, the feeling seemed to be that the international financial community would not permit yet another major market crash since it might create an unprecedented crisis that could set back emerging markets as an asset class by several years. This belief persisted up to the crash itself.

RUSSIA'S CONNECTION WITH THE OUTSIDE WORLD

There had been a belief among analysts that Russia was a 'law unto itself'. It was easier to connect other emerging market economies with one another, particularly through trade links as highlighted by South East Asia during the crash of 1997. Russia's participation in world trade was very small, amounting to a mere 1.4 per cent of the total world trade in 1997. Thus how much could the fate of other markets be tied to Russia's fate when they had little connection to its economy? What the analysts missed is that while the Russian economy might not have been highly integrated into the world economy, investors had highly integrated Russia into their investment world. Emerging markets had become globalized by the Asian crisis, whereas they had been largely distinct regions until then. Asian or Latin American problems would not have affected Eastern Europe as severely earlier in the 1990s. This inter-connection was also clear in the crisis aftermath: when Russia crashed, investors unwound positions in other parts of emerging markets to cover losses from Russian assets. Markets that had almost no economic connection with Russia (Greece is a good example) suffered severe declines simply to cover for Russia.

USES OF FOREIGN BOND PROCEEDS

At a road show for a particular Russian global bond issue, the use of the proceeds of the issue received a cursory mention both in the prospectus and in the Russian government's presentation. The bond proceeds were going to be used to plug holes in the budget. Russia is not the first country to use a bond's proceeds for fiscal support. However, there was something unsettling that Russia was using the quick fix of a large bond issue while continuing to avoid meaningful fiscal and structural reform. The Russian government appeared to be pursuing a short-sighted policy of propping itself up for now and worrying about the consequences later. Despite this obvious reality, analysts were eager to promote the global bond issues, and foreign investors were eager to buy them.

CONCLUSION

In hindsight, applying Western economic measures to the Russian economy as soon as a year after the end of the Soviet Union was premature. They did not truly describe the economy. A much greater knowledge of the Soviet economy and how it must affect the emerging Russian economy would have been helpful, as it would have explained economic relations in terms of structure and function. If analysts had understood the importance of control over natural resources right at the beginning of the 1990s, perhaps we would have had some inkling that the old established Soviet industrial élite was in a position to maintain much of its position and that the newcomers would maintain many of the practices of the old nomenklatura. The fact that fraud and deceit were very common in the old Soviet system helped prolong and encourage corruption in successive Russian governments and in the executive branch. The weakness of central government also greatly contributed to the corruption that eventually crushed the market in 1998. But analysts tended to gloss over or not appreciate the weakness of central government.

While the underpinnings of the crash were economic, as the GKO crisis showed, the timing and manner of the crash on August 17 were political. The manner in which the Russian government defaulted and devalued the currency – an abrupt announcement just a few days after the government had promised not to default – brought the question of political will back into the Russian risk premium. Probably the biggest issue that outside analysts missed was that political will was always a major risk factor with Russia, and that the general Russia delusion of the mid-1990s had obscured this fact.

Note

[1] Any views and analyses expressed in this chapter should not be assigned to a specific institution to which the author is affiliated.

6

CORPORATE GOVERNANCE IN RUSSIA: THE BATTLE FOR SHAREHOLDERS' RIGHTS

MARK MOBIUS AND ROMAN FILATOV[1]

A T TEMPLETON, STARTING WITH OUR FIRST EMERGING markets fund in 1987, we have been buffeted by the waves of emerging market crisis, price booms and crashes, restructuring stories and shareholder abuses. But the number and scope of corporate governance violations in Russia is appalling. Russia has certainly not been the safest market to invest based on economic and political criteria, but it has become infamous for the huge number of minority shareholder rights abuses perpetrated by the voracious and corrupted company managements and controlling shareholders. An enormous amount of value has been transferred from companies' coffers to controlling managers and shareholders even when they have not had the majority of the shares, thus reducing the attractiveness of Russian capital markets for minority investors and particularly foreign minority investors. Without foreign minority investors such as pension funds and other institutional investors in addition to the wealthy Russians and Russian companies which prefer to invest their money outside of Russia, it is going to be very difficult for the country to have high and sustainable growth in the long run.

The 1998 crisis proved the need to create a system of governance and control satisfactory for investors. Before that crisis, when investors were euphoric over skyrocketing stock prices, there was little talk about corporate governance. Everyone was excited about Russia and investors were greedily scooping up Russian stocks, not paying enough attention to the quality of management and their practices within the company. Speculators were not taking any active part in overseeing company activities, and management of many companies were feeling free and uncontrolled to help themselves to company assets. These managers would laugh at you if you started to talk about manager accountability to shareholders. They still do, but perhaps in the closet and not to our faces.

Although the number of Russian companies listed on stock exchanges and registered with share registrars amounts to roughly 250, trading on the Russian markets is concentrated in a handful of companies, most of which are in the natural resources sector such as minerals, petroleum and gas, as well as utilities such as electric power and telecommunications. With the rouble devaluation at the end of 1998 and high commodity prices in 1999–2000, the mining and oil companies have become very profitable so that there has been little incentive on their part to attract new outside capital from shareholders and thus to change their corporate governance practices. It must be conceded, however, that some Russian companies have started to change for the better, the reason being that controlling shareholders of those companies are beginning to realize that there could be more security for their share ownership if they gain respectability inside and outside of Russia and if their stock is listed in the U.S. and other major markets.

Nevertheless, the theft goes on. There are several ways Russian companies have violated shareholder rights.

THE BATTLE

Transfer pricing and theft of earnings

This is one of the most popular types of violations. Many companies, especially export and import-oriented firms, divert cashflows to affiliated companies controlled by the owner/managers, such as offshore structures and trading vehicles, or holding companies. In the oil industry a great number of production subsidiaries of oil holdings have been stripped of profits this way. For example, after Yukos took over its

66 Many companies, especially export and import-oriented firms, divert cashflows to affiliated companies controlled by the owner/managers **99**

main production subsidiaries Tomskneft, Yuganskneftegaz and Samaraneftegaz B, it forced them to sell oil to the holding company and related trading subsidiaries at unfairly low prices, leaving the subsidiaries with costs and unpaid debts. In the shareholders' meeting in the spring of 1999 Yukos tried to force Tomskneft shareholders to approve those prices. But since transfer pricing is possible in the case of oil companies at two levels – at the holding company level and trading companies level – shareholders of the holding oil companies are not safeguarded from such murky transactions. Transfer pricing helps companies minimize taxes, but the problem is that the profits end up in the pockets of a major shareholder or a small group of managers, and minority investors get nothing.

Transfer of assets

Theft of assets, including transactions with interested parties, is also widely used. According to Russian law the boards of directors have a great deal of discretion over company's assets, e.g. the board can authorize divestiture of up to 25 per cent of company assets without shareholder approval. General directors have substantial power as well. As most boards of directors consist of insiders, it presents almost no problem for the management to form a couple of shell companies and sell some assets to them quite cheaply.

One of the most prominent scandals was related to the proposed restructuring programme of Unified Energy Systems (UES). Initially, the management of the company proposed to break the holding company and separate generating and distribution by creating several hundred new companies, thus robbing UES of its main assets by selling assets where there was no market for them, not independent valuators, and leaving a wide opportunity for asset stripping. We believe some crucial problems of the sector should be solved first, such as tariff reform, elimination of cross-subsidization, and elimination of non-payments. Fortunately, thanks to the pressure from minority investors, that plan has been revised; nevertheless the problem of UES restructuring is on the agenda and negotiations with the government are proceeding to form a mutually acceptable plan on how to protect integrity of the electricity network and make sure there are no violations of minority investors' rights.

Dilution

Many violations in Russia have been via additional share issues, the main purpose of which was not to raise capital for the company but to dilute minority shareholders under unfair conditions. The placement terms of issues are usually structured in such a way as to exclude existing shareholders from purchasing proportionate shares of the new issues. In most cases new issues have been placed with one or several shareholders related to the management and/or majority shareholder. Examples of this would be the oil company Yukos where dilutions were executed in its subsidiaries, and another oil company Sidanco with its attempted share issue. Share placement prices often had nothing to do with actual market prices. Transfer pricing/asset stripping and dilutions frequently go in hand. Management decreases the attractiveness of the company via transfer pricing and when stock prices fall, they do dilutive share issues to themselves (disguised in dummy companies, of course, gaining majority or full control at no or little expense to themselves).

Destroying dissent

A common practice is to ban some shareholders from participating in shareholders' meetings. Some groups use various methods to prevent other shareholders from attending and voting on important items on the agenda. This can be facilitated by filing a lawsuit against an 'enemy' shareholder so that his shares are arrested and cannot be voted. The court hearing can be appointed in three months, while the shareholders' meeting is conducted in one month. Again, Yukos is perhaps the most experienced large company in this type of violation. Yukos's fight with Dart Management soon after the 1998 crisis continued for a long time with lawsuits filed on both sides, and received a lot of publicity both in Russia and abroad.

Fabricated bankruptcies

Fabricated bankruptcies occur when a group of managers, investors or creditors put the company, which is viable and attractive to them, into bankruptcy proceedings. Usually an outside management team is appointed by a court and somehow often it turns out that the managers are related to the group which initiated the proceedings. The stock price then falls and shares can be easily bought from panicking shareholders. In this case control over company cashflows may be gained without much investment. BP Amoco was fighting for control over Sidanco and one of its major production subsidiaries, Chernogorneft. Due to poor corporate governance practices on the side of Sidanco and Chernogorneft, the latter was left with substantial debts and no means to repay them. Another Russian oil company, TNK, launched a hostile takeover attack on Chernogorneft, buying out the company's debt and initiating bankruptcy proceedings against it to buy the company.

Registrar abuses

Several years ago many companies had their affiliated registrars, which allowed them to control and influence share trading. There have even been cases in which shareholders were wiped off from registrars as if they had never existed.

Withholding information and lack of transparency

Disclosure of company information has been lacking for as long as the Russian stock market has existed. Company directors have consistently restricted access of minority shareholders to information about company activities such as production statistics, debt structure ownership structure and, most of all, meaningful financial information. Company managements become particularly sensitive when questions are raised regarding the ownership structure and the question of who actually controls the company. Sibneft, for example, has not disclosed its ownership structure despite persistent inquiries from minority shareholders and investors. Beneficial owners are hidden behind an impenetrable wall of offshore companies and nominees.

In some of the abovementioned cases foreign fund managers were the victims, as with Tomskneft which was raided by Yukos, resulting in Tomskneft's market capitalization falling from triple-digit to single-digit figures. This example illustrated almost every conceivable type of minority rights violation – transfer pricing, asset transferring, and dilution. Ultimately, foreign investors were left with an illiquid penny stock, for which there was only one buyer.

One of the most recent examples was the 'restructuring story' of Norilsk Nickel. Though restructuring *per se* was needed, when it started the company was in no way investor-friendly or transparent. At the beginning of 2000 the company acquired UK-based metal trading company Norimet for a consideration of a large stake in Norilsk Nickel's main subsidiary without any approval or notification of shareholders. Furthermore, Norimet's valuation was questionable. More importantly the metal trader was believed to be associated with the management of Norilsk Nickel, who then proceeded to complete a 'restructuring' which they said would be 'beneficial' to minority investors. Of course, this was not the case since minority investors, including foreign investors, saw 10 per cent of the company's equity taken away from them in the transaction.

FIGHTING BACK

The situation is gradually changing and corporate governance is under scrutiny from investors and government authorities. The Federal Securities Commission (FSC) seems to be taking a more aggressive role in pursuing companies which violate shareholder rights. The FSC has achieved some positive results on information disclosure by forcing companies to publish quarterly reports. In the spring of 1999 it obtained the right to fine and initiate court proceedings against those companies which missed reporting deadlines. However, we believe that the FSC is generally still toothless and should be granted more powers to fine and punish violators. The sad fact is that we cannot rely on the FSC to defend investor rights because laws are unclear and law enforcement is ineffective.

At the end of 1998 the Co-ordination Centre for Protection of Investor Rights was launched, with the main purpose of monitoring corporate actions and identifying and pursuing corporate governance violations or potential shareholder rights problems. NAUFOR (the National

Association of Stock Market Participants) and several major asset management companies, including Templeton, were initial supporters of the centre, now called the Association for Protection of Investors. One of the association's first large-scale projects was co-ordination and consolidation of minority stakes of a number of larger investors so as to appoint minority shareholder representatives to the board of major companies. There have also been a number of successful projects and actions which have stopped violations.

The major task lying ahead of the government and investors is to obtain action in the legislature to enact laws which would prohibit insider dealings, improve information disclosure, provide for the ability of investors and government agencies to fire and sue managers and directors of a company, put more control and transparency on related party transactions, including transfer pricing and asset stripping, and change the criminal code to provide for criminal proceedings against violators. On top of that investors are being urged to be more proactive in defending their interests and those of their shareholders by pursuing managers and companies with bad corporate governance practices.

66 The major task lying ahead of the government and investors is to obtain action in the legislature to enact laws which would prohibit insider dealings 99

Progress in the legislature area has been proceeding at a snail's pace. Although government action is key to improving corporate governance, up to now the state has been indifferent to shareholder abuses and not taken due care of its own assets even though the government is a shareholder in many enterprises and has been subject to the same minority rights violations as all the other minority shareholders. Many foreign investors and Russians feel the state should look urgently at the problem of corporate governance and clarify laws and procedures.

Proper corporate governance is essential for Russia to be an integrated part of the global economy and capital markets. Without good corporate governance Russian markets will remain highly speculative, undercapitalized and volatile, with short-term investment horizons, thus holding back growth and prosperity. With its huge land mass, large population and abundant natural resources the country could become one of the fastest-developing economies, attracting a great deal of long-term capital and delivering excellent results. But this promise will remain unfulfilled unless good corporate governance and the protection of minority shareholders are improved.

Note

[1] Any views and analyses expressed in this chapter should not be assigned to a specific institution to which the authors are affiliated.

7

SMALL ENTERPRISES IN RUSSIA: SURVIVING THE CRISIS?

STEPHAN BOVEN[1]

THE DOMESTIC DEFAULT OF THE GOVERNMENT, the dramatic devaluation of the rouble and the collapse of a number of Russian banks undoubtedly had a severe impact on the business environment in Russia and its enterprise sector. Many companies, both small and large, lost their trade relationships, had their current accounts frozen in bankrupt banks and experienced problems servicing their hard-currency obligations. However, the swift recovery of the real economy gave some indication that the impact on the enterprise sector as a whole was not as severe as may have been assumed immediately after the crisis. This seems especially true for the micro and small enterprise (MSE) sector. The experience of the Russia Small Business Fund (RSBF), an MSE lending project, and the performance of its loan portfolio provide strong evidence that the often-assumed flexibility of the MSE sector was indeed proven in the Russian crisis.

LENDING UNDER THE RUSSIA SMALL BUSINESS FUND – THE PRE-CRISIS SITUATION

The RSBF started its activities in March 1994 and is the largest lending project of its kind in Eastern Europe. Under the RSBF the European

Bank of Reconstruction and Development, supported by a major contribution from the G7 countries,[2] provides bank-to-bank finance to Russian partner banks for on-lending to private MSEs. The partner banks bear the full credit risk for sub-loans. The financial offer is combined with significant technical assistance to implement a suitable credit technology to ensure commercially viable lending activities. For this purpose, the work of expatriate and local credit advisors focuses on the introduction of customer-oriented and efficient lending procedures with reduced bureaucratic obstacles. Lending decisions are cashflow based, replacing the former asset- (i.e. collateral-) based lending practices. Instead of the availability of collateral and a large number of required documents, the debt capacity of a given client becomes the basis for a positive credit decision.

The RSBF has two major credit products: micro loans and small loans. Micro loans are offered to sole proprietors and companies with up to 20 employees in amounts up to $20,000. For small loans the ceiling is set at $125,000 for companies with up to 100 employees. Loans have a maturity of up to three years and can be used for investment and working capital purposes. Whereas micro loans are disbursed in roubles or US dollars, small loans are mostly denominated in or indexed to the US dollar. The interest rates charged to sub-borrowers are set by the partner banks at commercial levels based on market considerations and individual risk assessment. RSBF loans are typically disbursed as fixed-instalment loans with combined interest and principal. However, short grace periods and seasonal adjustments to payment plans are applied if necessary.

The RSBF started its operations in three pilot regions, Tula, Nizhny Novgorod and Tomsk. These cities were chosen because they were especially affected by the disintegration of the military-industrial complex of the former Soviet Union. After an initial training period for loan officers, the first loan was disbursed in March 1994. In January 1995, the project began to expand into new regions and by the end of June 1998 the RSBF was operating in 23 regions across the whole of Russia.[3] The RSBF had achieved broad regional coverage, operating in St Petersburg as well as Central Russia (Samara, Togliatti), the Urals (Ekaterinburg, Chelyabinsk), Siberia (Novosibirsk, Kemerovo, Barnaul,

Krasnoyarsk) and also in the Far East (Vladivostok, Khabarovsk). As of June 1998, the loan portfolio of the RSBF had the characteristics outlined in Table 7.1.

As planned from the outset, the project covered the full range of micro and small enterprises with no lower limit applied. The majority of borrowers were very small businesses with up to five employees or single entrepreneurs, and micro loans were disbursed in amounts as small as $50. The average loan amount outstanding grew over time, starting from approximately $3000 in 1994 to above $13,500 in 1998, reflecting a stabilizing (pre-crisis) economy and the higher credit demands of repeat customers.

Because small loans dominated the portfolio in terms of volume, nearly 65 per cent of the volume outstanding was denominated in US dollars. The loan portfolio was of very high quality, with only 2.51 per cent in arrears (>30 days, portfolio at risk) and accumulated loan losses amounted to less than 0.5 per cent of total volume disbursed. The portfolio was evenly distributed across the regions, with concentrations in Moscow (21.4 per cent of outstanding volume) and Nizhny Novgorod (18.4 per cent of loans outstanding).

Table 7.1 *RSBF portfolio summary as of June 1998*

	Number of loans	Volume ($ million)	Average loan amount ($)
Total portfolio	6638	93.2	13,538
of which			
Micro loans	*5310*	*33.8*	*6372*
Small loans	1328	59.4	44,709
of which			
Rouble loans	*4773*	*29.2*	*6118*
US dollar loans	1865	64.0	34,311
Arrears (portfolio at risk, >30days)*			
Micro loans		1.6%	
Small loans		3.0%	

Source: RSBF statistics

* This figure includes the total amount of principal outstanding of any loan with any kind of overdue payments (principal or interest).

Two years later, the figures for July 2000 show an increase in the number of borrowers, but at the same time a much-reduced average loan size, resulting in a much smaller volume outstanding (see Table 7.2). This reflects the reduced debt capacity of most RSBF borrowers. As a consequence the share of micro loans in the RSBF portfolio increased markedly. In line with the increased share of micro loans, the share of rouble-denominated loans also increased, although more than 50 per cent of all loans outstanding were still in dollars. Most importantly, however, arrears rates were at or close to pre-crisis levels, and accumulated loan losses (for the period from 1994 to 2000) stayed below 0.7 per cent of the total amount disbursed by those five banks that survived the crisis.

Despite some changes, the distribution by industry shows a domination of trade activities in both the pre- and post-crisis portfolio, which is as much a result of the industry structure of the former Soviet Union as of the country's development since 1989 (see Figure 7.1).

In the former Soviet Union, services in general and trade in particular were seen merely as necessary supports to the production process. Consequently, the distribution network was underdeveloped. Moreover, many shops and outlets collapsed due to the disruption of distribution channels during the break-up of the Soviet Union. This gap was quickly filled by a large number of small traders. Trading activities involved low entry barriers, i.e. limited entrepreneurial skills and capital input, and even small operations could provide sufficient income. At the same time, many people were forced into self-employment in order to secure an income for their families.[4]

Table 7.2 *RSBF portfolio summary as of July 2000*

	Number of loans	Volume ($ million)	Average loan amount ($)
Total portfolio	7412	59.6	8841
Micro loans	6664	25.8	3867
Small loans	696	30.8	44,294
Rouble loans	6367	28.7	4513
US-dollar loans	1045	30.9	29,577
Arrears (portfolio at risk, >30days)			
Micro loans		1.3%	
Small loans		4.2%	

Source: RSBF statistics

Figure 7.1 *Distribution of clients by industry (comparison 1998–2000)*

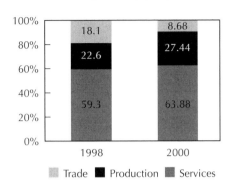

Source: RSBF statistics

By contrast, the establishment of production companies was far more difficult, not only because of the management skills and larger amounts of capital needed but also because these companies were facing the double competition of Western imports and existing state-owned monopolists. This overall development was clearly reflected in the loan portfolio of the RSBF.

The crisis of 1998 led to changes in the sector structure of the portfolio. There was an increase in the share of trade, due to the appearance of a large number of new micro enterprises. Many employees lost their savings due to the crisis and saw salaries owed to them by large enterprises devalue dramatically in dollar terms (wage arrears of more than six months were not uncommon). The effect of the crisis was therefore to persuade even more Russians that establishing their own small business offered a genuine alternative to employment, which provided only a low and irregular income. The micro enterprise sector can be considered an important stabilising factor, especially in depressed regions like the Siberian Kuzbass. Starting a business, usually small-scale trade activities, was one way out of frustration and dependence.

❝many shops and outlets collapsed due to the disruption of distribution channels during the break-up of the Soviet Union❞

The share of production companies in the loan portfolio also increased post-crisis, although the production sector gained less than expected from the reduced competition from Western imports. This is indicated by the development in the absolute number of outstanding loans to production companies, which decreased by 15 per cent. This result is at least partly explained by the fact that many production borrowers, especially in manufacturing, relied heavily on imported inputs and spare parts, some of which could not be replaced by local suppliers. Nonetheless, the negative trend was partly offset by producers in the food processing and textile industry, in which almost all input could be accessed locally or within CIS countries.

The only segment that clearly lost as a result of the crisis was the service sector. Before the crisis an increasing number of companies provided services for the developing Russian middle class. This included businesses as diverse as restaurants and pubs, hairdressers, dry cleaners, and medical and dental services. The decline in real income led to reduced spending particularly in consumer services. Whereas traders could compensate for the shift in demand for clothing and food by changing their product mix, service companies had no such alternative and were faced with falling turnover and financial difficulties.

In sum, the comparison between June 1998 and July 2000 shows a further expansion in the number of RSBF borrowers. An ever increasing number of micro enterprises, single entrepreneurs and very small enterprises were using the loans offered under the programme as a source of finance. The increased number of borrowers could not offset the reduction in loan volume, which was caused by the greatly reduced debt capacity of the individual borrower. Most importantly, however, the loan portfolio before and after the crisis showed an exceptionally high quality, with low arrears rates and very limited loan losses. Whereas lending to small enterprises is usually considered high risk, especially in difficult environments like Russia, the lending results of the RSBF, despite the problems experienced in 1998/9, contradict this assumption. This can be attributed partly to the lending approach and the credit technology applied within the RSBF, but it also demonstrates that Russian small businesses not only have the capacity to repay their loan obligations but, even more importantly, they also have the willingness to do so.

THE RUSSIAN CRISIS – ROUBLE DEVALUATION, BANK BANKRUPTCY AND LOAN RECOVERY

In the immediate aftermath of the crisis there were fears of loan losses of more than 50 per cent or even the total collapse of project activities. First, two-thirds of the RSBF loan portfolio was denominated in US dollars. Second, all of the RSBF's partner banks operating nationwide, with the exception of state-owned Sberbank, collapsed in the crisis. These banks accounted for approximately 60 per cent of the outstanding portfolio. It was assumed that borrowers, which were in any case barely able to service their quadrupled debt in rouble terms, would lose any incentive to repay when their lender became bankrupt. In reality, however, the portfolio developed rather differently.

The first reaction of all partner banks to the crisis was a drastic slowdown of all lending activities in August 1998, irrespective of the type of borrower, loan amount or currency (see Table 7.3). The portfolio experienced a decline of approximately 40 per cent between July and December 1998, despite the fact that $15.5 million of new loans were still disbursed between August and December. Decline in the dollar-denominated small loan portfolio alone amounted to $16.1 million, so the reduction is only partly explained by the impact of devaluation on the rouble-denominated loan portfolio (this effect can be estimated at $20 million). The key factor was that more than $30 million of outstanding loans were repaid over the same period, meaning that a large number of clients not only met their repayment schedules but also prepaid significant portions of their exposure, given that further devaluation of the rouble was expected.

With respect to loan-portfolio quality, the initial increase of arrears was limited, but in October 1998 payment problems became more visible and the arrears rate reached more than 10 per cent by the end of 1998.

Table 7.3 *RSBF lending statistics*

1998/9	No. of loans granted	Dollar amount of loans granted	No. of loans outstanding	Dollar amount outstanding	Arrears in % (>30 days, active banks)
Dec 1997	1133	17,473,143	5702	77,801,894	1.6
1998					
March	932	14,069,518	5986	79,659,274	2.5
June	890	16,606,668	6638	93,211,622	2.5
September	57	430,068	6125	70,775,740	4.7
December	448	3,537,787	4925	60,891,821	10.7
1999					
March	465	3,657,540	4428	54,794,982	10.7
June	524	4,573,211	4372	52,233,142	11.6
September	692	5,637,294	4849	52,949,809	5.8
December	1007	9,356,718	5716	58,459,470	4.7

Source: RSBF statistics

However, only in January/February 1999 was the full impact of the crisis felt. January had traditionally been a month of increased arrears due to reduced economic activity and sales, particularly in the retail sector. January 1999 showed a similar picture, but on a much larger scale. The holiday season between the end of December and mid-January and the resulting sales peak had enabled many companies to keep up with their loan repayments in previous years. And typically, the December peak had also enabled most businesses to cope with the slow January. However in 1998–9, this was not the case as December income was spent on loan repayment. Reduced sales after the holiday period then resulted in many businesses being unable to service their debt. Accordingly, the arrears share of the RSBF loan portfolio reached its highest level in February 1999 (14.1 per cent).

The immediate reaction of RSBF staff and partner banks was to maintain even closer contact with the borrowers and a repeat analysis of all clients was performed. It showed that not only dollar borrowers but also rouble borrowers were facing serious problems. For the latter, although the outstanding loan amount had dropped in dollar terms, it was fairly stable in real terms due to the low level of inflation. At the same time, borrowers faced a sharp drop in their sales even in nominal (rouble) terms. Moreover, retail traders suffered from a practical stand-still of the supply chain since wholesalers were unable to set the correct selling prices and refused to deliver any goods.

Worst hit by the crisis were companies relying on Western imports in their business activities, such as trading companies importing tele-comunications, computer and other technical equipment. These companies faced immediate problems as they could neither change to local supply nor were they able to adjust their prices. In addition, those suppliers which continued to deliver were asking for prepayment for goods supplied. Many producers and manufacturers were also relying on Western components and spare parts. Their current stock gave them only limited time to find alternative sources or different technical solutions for their line of production.

Nonetheless, not all clients were struggling for survival. The RSBF credit technology based the decision to grant a loan predominantly on payment capacity at the time of the loan application. In the difficult Russian context this amounted to a requirement that in general a client should be able to repay their loan even if the borrowed funds were lost completely, i.e. the financed project or transaction failed. Of course, the additional working capital or investment more often than not generated additional income, which put the borrower in a stronger financial position than before the loan disbursement. As indicated by the decline of the RSBF portfolio described above, a substantial number of RSBF borrowers had sufficient reserves not only to keep up with their payment schedule but also to prepay a large part of their loans. The conservative lending approach used in the RSBF explains partly why, even in January/February, nearly 90 per cent of all clients were able to service their loans in accordance with the agreed repayment schedule.

In all cases where the renewed credit analysis revealed that a customer was unable to meet their obligations under the loan agreement, different approaches were adopted to ensure loan recovery. If the payment problems were considered to be of a temporary nature, a new repayment schedule within the original life of the loan was adopted. A permanent drop in the debt capacity of a client, however, required a reduction in the monthly instalments and extension of the loan maturity. In some cases, these adjustments were connected with the question

❝In a fast-changing and unstable environment like Russia, the reputation risk resulting from a default is very limited❞

of collateral. Whenever possible, additional collateral was taken in return for the improved loan terms. With some borrowers, an agreed sale of (pledged) assets not required for business purposes was an appropriate option to reduce the overall debt burden of a company without affecting its payment capacity. However, all measures taken relied on a key assumption: the willingness of the client to repay.

This assumption was far from clear-cut in Russia. In a Western context, the general willingness to service an obligation can be assumed due to the reputation risks and the legal consequences of a loan default, most of all in respect to the collateral pledged. In comparison, a Russian borrower faced only limited consequences. In a fast-changing and unstable environment like Russia, the reputation risk resulting from a default is very limited, especially on a bank loan, as Russian banks generally had (and still have) a bad reputation based on poor business practice and a lack of customer orientation. At the same time, Russia still suffers from a weak legal system, with only limited protection for creditors. Enforcement of collateral is slow and the result often unpredictable. And, especially for legal entities, asset stripping would have taken a matter of days in the absence of central registration for collateral other than real estate. Nevertheless, the number of RSBF clients choosing this option was extremely small.

The quick reaction of RSBF staff and the co-operative approach used in negotiations with clients served as an effective tool, partly offsetting the lack of leverage provided by reputation risk and the legal system. As important as the recovery efforts was the prospect of continued access to loans. The clients kept repaying their loans largely in order to secure future finance. Close contact and discussion with the borrower and a flexible approach were of utmost importance for loan recovery. Loan enforcement that would lead to the financial collapse of a borrower would have been counterproductive even if the borrower owned sufficient assets to cover the loan, as they would lose any incentive to repay. Instead, the borrower would try to defend themselves in court and in the meantime secure their assets by shifting them to other companies.

The offer of future co-operation under the RSBF was credible and valuable for its borrowers because of the success in implementing a credit approach that was clearly distinct from usual Russian bank practice. The latter was characterized by high collateral requirements, inefficient and bureaucratic procedures and a decision-making process that was mostly dependent on individuals acting at their own discretion. Small businesses in particular faced serious obstacles in receiving any kind of finance. If accepted at all by a bank, the owner-manager had to abandon their business for days to obtain all documents required. At the same time, they would struggle to provide sufficient collateral as business assets were usually not accepted at all due to enforcement problems. The impact of collateral requirements was magnified because banks required from small businesses far more collateral than usual, as they were unable to perform a realistic assessment of the borrowers' credit worthiness. Thus, in their lending they were almost entirely dependent on the collateral. And even if the owner of a small business could cope with these problems, actually receiving a loan could still be problematic. With no interest in lending to small businesses, banks' decision making and disbursement were very slow and applications were rejected without explanation.

In contrast, the RSBF aims for quick and customer-orientated procedures, document requirements that are kept to a minimum and a transparent decision-making process. Loans are disbursed in the easiest way possible, often in cash for small loan amounts, without the necessity to open an account. These measures are not only for the benefit of the client, but at the same time increase efficiency within the banks. Increased efficiency and reduced costs are a precondition for profitable lending activities. The credit technology used in analyzing clients enables the loan officer to receive a realistic picture of the financial position of a borrower and to estimate their debt capacity. At the same time, this serves as a basis for the lending decision and makes the approach to collateral much more flexible. The partner banks are trained to be able to rely on a client's cashflow instead of their assets, i.e. their collateral.

The final important element of the lending approach is the close client relationship and the graduation principle. To limit credit risk while at the same time increasing the number of eligible borrowers, the terms and conditions for loans are initially quite restrictive and are relaxed as the client relationship develops. At the same time, clients are contacted regularly, not only for monitoring purposes but also as an opportunity to discuss future needs for finance. As a result a regular and ongoing client relationship is actively developed. These features enabled the RSBF to give a credible offer to borrowers to begin with and also served the programme well when borrowers were struggling with their payments in the aftermath of the crisis.

Although to a lesser extent, these principles also worked for those banks that failed in the crisis and were put under external supervision. Although no more lending could reasonably be expected by borrowers from these banks, most of the outstanding RSBF portfolio was nevertheless recovered. This was possible because of the assignment agreements in place with the partner banks, which gave the EBRD the right to transfer the portfolios either to itself or to other nominated banks. A large proportion of sub-loans was transferred to an EBRD- controlled Russian bank, which was staffed with trained RSBF personnel, in order to continue the monitoring process and finance new applications. In most cases, even the (now jobless) loan officers of the failed bank were employed by this bank, in which case the client relationship was kept fully intact.

CONCLUSION

It is clear that in small business lending the stability of the institution and the credibility of a long-term partnership with borrowers are key factors. These are not only preconditions for successful lending operations to small business in general but can make a decisive difference in crisis situations. Only a lending institution that can keep the promise of being a reliable source of finance to small enterprises can expect its borrowers to stick to the relationship even in difficult times. As long as this prospect is kept intact, the lending institution has a chance to cope with difficult situations that have a negative impact on its loan portfolio.

As the Russian crisis has demonstrated, the majority of small businesses are able to absorb even massive shocks. They quickly adjust their product range, find new suppliers and are often able to rely on their own savings or on their social network to overcome their problems. The ability to service a loan, however, is not enough, as the often cited flexibility of small businesses can easily turn against the lender. Therefore, in environments where the lender cannot rely on the legal framework and collateral as an incentive for loan repayment, there must be a different incentive, which ultimately can only be the prospect of an ongoing relationship with the lender and access to future finance. Only this prospect makes it worthwhile for the borrower to repay a loan in a situation in which the lending institution can easily be overwhelmed by a mass default of its borrowers.

Notes

[1] Any views and analyses expressed in this chapter should not be assigned to a specific institution to which the author is affiliated.

[2] This has been supplemented by the EU TACIS and Switzerland.

[3] Of these, eight started only in 1998.

[4] For women in particular this was often the motivation to start small trade operations – 60 per cent of all businesses applying for a loan of less than $3000 are owned by women, whereas in the overall portfolio male ownership dominates to the same degree (60 per cent).

PART III

Moving the frontier

8

BUBBLE

AL BREACH[1]

RUSSIA – THE TRUE PICTURE

A HUGE EUROPEAN COUNTRY with a brilliant but deeply troubled history finally decides to put an end to its quixotic, expansionist militarist adventures to (re-?) join its former adversaries in the free world, building prosperity through capitalism and liberal market democracy. With an educated, extremely cheap workforce, massive natural wealth, and a huge amount of catch-up in all spheres possible, the economy, managed by a team of smart young reformers following in the 'transition' footsteps of former satellites to the West, is set to grow at rapid rates. Big profits will be made, and investors would be mad to miss out on the rapidly appreciating financial assets of what will be one of the world's biggest markets in coming decades.

Or

A deeply corrupt country, run by an 'élite' with no regard for its people, no experience of sticking to the laws it writes, and a history of default second to none. The capitalism, which this élite is constructing, is that of a kleptocracy where the well-connected classes steal from the poorly connected and anyone mad enough to lend them or 'invest' any money. Investors should simply take the unheeded advice of the mother of a second generation émigré, one of the boom's most successful profiteers,[2] who joked at the height of the euphoria: 'My mother always told me never to invest in Russia!'

Each of these two factual views (factual in the sense that no actual lies are included, and who ever knows which one will be 'ultimately' true?) dominated with an interval of less than 18 months: spring/summer 1997, winter 1998/9. Each accounted for large sales of Russian assets, first by Russians to foreigners, then by foreigners to Russians (the second time around these were 'large' sales, if we discount the small matter of asset price deflation). And each view was spouted and believed by many sane, 'rational' investors and commentators.

The result, of course, was one of the most spectacular booms, followed by one of the most spectacular busts in history.

HOW?

How can so many smart investors and commentators have been duped twice (twice, since the first time they bought high and the second time sold low)? How can such a reversal in sentiment be explained inside any remotely rationalistic paradigm of the way the world works? Simply put, how can it have happened?

Before trying to sketch some answers to these questions I need to stress what is still a contested point. I hold not only that the first of the two views paraphrased above has been proved wrong, but that the second has been, or at least will be, proved wrong too. Some will disagree, but I contend that the excellent economic news coming out of Russia now will continue long enough for history – and asset prices – to judge that the first view was also kind of right. In any case, I repeat: *both* views contain much truth, though not enough for a full explanation.

And so, back to those 'how' questions. First the obvious and central answer.

Ignorance

There was lots of it, and on all sides. Policymakers in the dark – Hayekian lovers of free markets that they had never known or seen operate, former Communists who believed way too much of their own propaganda about Russia's superiority, Russian economists and advisors who were expert in the workings of the real economy[3] but were beginners on the working of financial markets, foreign advisors in the dark – the IMF had experience of balance-of-payment crises in the developed world, but not of fiscal and systemic transitions. In short, no one involved really knew the measure of what it was all about.

And of course commentators and we Western investors did not know *anything*. Here was a previously totally closed country suddenly opened up to an uncomprehending outside world (it did not help that the few Western scholars of the place were mainly Kremlinologists, trained in reading the configuration of Politburo members on Lenin's tomb rather than in either socialist or market economics). This massive country was doing something that our countries had never dreamt of doing – shifting in ten years to the model which we had reached organically over hundreds of years. Perhaps the most confusing thing was that we thought we understood *our* model: the chaotic situation that developed in Russia revealed the importance of all kinds of underlying structures and institutions that most of us in the West generally fail to notice or take for granted.[4]

In a sense this sea of ignorance is not surprising: Russia's reform was the biggest fiscal contraction/turnaround in the history of economics – a turn in the budget of almost 40 per cent of GDP (1991–2000), and a contraction in spending of similar proportions. Put another way, in more general terms, the real ignorance was about just how bad things were in 1991 when the wheels fell off the Soviet juggernaut. The country was bankrupt in every conceivable sense: financially, ecnomically, politically and morally. And this was not understood. How could a nation that had been a feared superpower only yesterday be so decrepit? How could the core of that super-state, which looked so strong, turn out to be a mirage? Only today do I understand just how little control was held by the Central Committee in the dying days of the USSR and by the nascent Russian government at the beginning of Yeltsin's presidency – the state, and with it the power structure, literally crumbled.

The answers to the riddle of Soviet collapse lie in the huge lack of self-knowledge and self-analysis in the Soviet system – no one was allowed to systematically work on what ailed the place, instead they were made to churn out propaganda. To paraphrase one observer: Russia was 'the most hypocritical society in the world' under the Soviets. The same observer went on to say that it turned in the early 1990s into 'the most cynical' society in the world. The Communist élite with their absolute power were utterly corrupt and by the end had *no* sense of legitimate progress, but they were the only group with their hands on the controls. So the cynicism, total malaise and absolute corruption combined to create a real cesspit. Most Western observers had no understanding of quite what a cesspit it was, and viewed Russian politics with a simplified Western gloss, when what was really occurring was a wild revolution.

> **"Russia's reform was the biggest fiscal contraction/turnaround in the history of economics"**

On a more practical level, everyone was hindered by the appalling data – in a place where prices were largely an accounting device and money was not money, what was to be expected? I recall, in the midst of the euphoria, standing in front of 20 or so fixed-income investors, saying in passing in the middle of something else, '...Well of course the fiscal crisis...' with no emphasis, and being stopped by one of them saying 'which fiscal crisis?' They were duped by a government that reported its deficits without the cost of interest it paid on its domestic debts – the very same GKOs that all these folk had invested such amounts in – and counted all the bartered goods and 'offsets' it received as revenues. The IMF is to blame here, I think – more transparency from the fund, which knew just how bad things were, would have helped.

Another, perhaps very important, piece of poor data was the balance of payments. One reason why the exchange rate was not considered over-valued was that the country ran a healthy current account surplus, at least according to the CBR's accounts. That current account surplus might well have disappeared if imports had been measured correctly – the gross amount spent by Russians abroad (a number that gets booked as a services import and therefore above the line) was booked at about $8 billion annually, but given what we know about Russians on the Côte d'Azur and in Versace shops in Paris, London, New York, etc., this number seems unrealistically low. If imports had been boosted by the full errors and emissions number (a residual left at the bottom of the capital account and caused by poor accounting) it would have eradicated the current account surplus. If imports had been boosted further by adding some of the formal 'capital flight' that simply got spent from bank accounts abroad, the current account would have shown a deficit. That would perhaps have been enough to silence some of the bullish reports.

Perhaps the single most crucial bit of ignorance concerned barter, offsets, veksels, arrears, non-payments – the whole 'virtual' shebang. No one understood this then (only a few enlightened souls concentrated on it, unfortunately not including me), and few, if any, do now. With hindsight though, it is clear that the settlement of so much 'business' in barter etc. made a mockery of the GDP numbers that we all used. GDP numbers are important: we all do our valuation ratios using them as the denominator. This virtual stuff, and particularly barter, came about, I believe, as a way for Russia's non-energy-rich industrial heartland to live with impossibly tight exchange rate and monetary policy. Without it they would have all been bankrupt. They used these surrogates to *inflate* the value of their revenues, and thus hide real losses. Using such inflated numbers meant that GDP was way too high. Supposing that 'real' (in some profound sense) GDP was half of the figure we were using at the time, critical ratios would have looked like this: debt/GDP >100 per cent, budget deficit 15 per cent or more of GDP, etc. How much money would have come in under these circumstances?

Thus at the heart of the lack of knowledge there was ignorance about prices – what anything in this new market was actually worth. The place was insufficiently a market economy to allow prices to perform the critical role that we ascribe to them in the West. The two most critical prices for investors – the exchange rate and asset prices – were tenuously connected with reality, resulting in what were (with hindsight) large over-valuations that eventually came crashing down in such spectacular fashion. The nebulousness of asset prices was in part a function of the fact that, even if companies really were making a lot of profits, being a minority investor did not guarantee the kind of rights we are now used to in the West. This is not surprising – how could Russians have been expected to graduate in one quick step to the (very) late 20th-century version of shareholder capitalism that we now (almost) take for granted?

Thus, while people agreed that the assets were worth something and that large amounts of money would be made (how could it not be so in a place with such huge mineral wealth, and with no war raging or war machine being primed?), no one knew how much, by whom or when.

Politics (or love of company)

Clearly, though, ignorance is not the whole story. On its own it should simply make people cautious. It does not go far in explaining why so much money was ploughed in. For that one has to look at the internal politics of the different sets of actors: the 'international community' (the IMF in particular), investors and investment banks and, of course, the Russians. All had their incentives, both on the way up and on the way down. And all the incentives fit with the old adage that it is better to run with the herd than piss against the wind.

The international community gave the job of helping its new friend Russia become the Russia we all wanted it to be to the IMF. No one wanted it to fail. This was an opportunity that, if not grabbed, might never be had again (whether or not this is true we will never know, but it felt true at the time). The IMF was hell-bent on success. Once it had its fingerprints all over Russia, it became its project. Unless it succeeded, the very existence of the IMF as an institution might be in question.

For investors and market participants it was more simple. Money was being made aplenty (the best-performing market in the world in most of 1996 and 1997). Even if you were a non-believer, you only had one of two options: sit it out and watch others get rich, or join in and hope. Since no one knew really whether it was true or not, it seemed quite likely that the train was leaving the station for good: it was now or never. So most chose now.

Once the crash had been and gone, the situation was reversed. If you invested in the place you had two perfectly correlated risks: markets performing badly, and being sacked. The only upside, for most non-shareholders, was that you might be 'lucky in a crap-shoot'. The risk-reward trade-off did not look good. Folks stayed out and sold low.

It was not that dissimilar for Russians. In the boom period you borrowed as much as you could (and there was lots on offer), used some of it for the better things in life and punted the rest on the stock market/GKO market/the rouble or whatever, since it all seemed like a one-way bet. Free money – if you miss out now, you will have missed out completely (including every tin-pot Russian region, which had an open invitation to go out and borrow). Post-crash, the herd logic worked the other way round. Why bother being virtuous and paying people back when everyone else is reneging on contracts and stealing the funds? Follow the crowd …

Emotions

But what drove the crowd? As ever with markets, two emotions were uppermost: greed and fear. First the former, then the latter. On everyone's part.

I felt deep down that something was amiss (failed to formulate it, of course) when a friend working as a broker described his experience with 'third-tier' stocks. He repeated the comment a number of times and it summed up the weirdness of the times: 'All I have to do is pick up the phone, mention some company in a place that no one has ever heard of before, including myself, and bang: I create value!' Not only did this illustrate the bonanza atmosphere, fuelled by the greed, but it also illustrates another point about the Russian boom: we were having our cake and eating it.

For as well as getting rich (or thinking we were), all of us actors – investors, Western officialdom, and also the Russians – desperately *wanted* Russia to succeed. The Evil Empire is won over to Good! (Good just happens to be us and our consumerist ways). And we were playing our part in winning it over. By investing money at outlandish interest rates or in outlandishly bad companies we were helping it succeed.

We, a post-Thatcher/Reagan generation who perhaps weren't quite as obsessed with money as our immediate elders, but sure liked the stuff, an eclectic bunch of capitalist misfits and profiteers, were 'doing good' at the same time as being paid ridiculous amounts of money.

Whether we knew it or not, we were all playing our parts in a big political battle for the country's soul, or at least for its direction. Yeltsin used this support and the money it brought, not for what it was intended (to help build Russia) but to help his cause, to win his battle by buying time and buying people over. Yeltsin is a contender for the title of most cognoscenti ringmaster in history. Just how cognoscenti he was will no doubt be debated for ever, but my vote is that, except when on the operating table or completely drunk (and maybe even then), he was a phenomenal force. *Everyone* of any intelligence and the slightest generosity who worked with him described him as politically brilliant. Indeed, how could he not have been, given that he rode, *and mastered*, that monster of a tumultuous decade?

> **66 Yeltsin is a contender for the title of most cognoscenti ringmaster in history. 99**

TABULA RASA *AND MARKETS' AVERSION TO 'EQUILIBRIA'*

I want to take a brief detour to theorize over what this tells us about markets and bubbles in general. The above 'answer' in terms of ignorance, politics and emotion goes some way to explaining what happened in Russia, but it is interesting to speculate about the more universal lessons of the Russian rollercoaster.

Two abstractions from the specifically Russian events are as follows: first, a critical element of any bubble seems to be a deep indeterminacy of asset prices, i.e. that some kind of *tabula rasa* is needed, on which two starkly opposing views can compete. Second, that markets, particularly such indeterminate ones, do not like 'equilibria' for long. I take these points in turn.

Tabula rasa

The two views of Russia outlined at the beginning of this chapter are perhaps caricatures, but they have an essence of truth. There can be two opposing views of any country at any time. But what made such a dichotomy so applicable to Russia at this time was that views on Russia could be – and were – written on something of a *tabula rasa*. There was little relevant history or past experience of capitalism and asset markets.

This lack of relevant history and experience meant there was little historical data with which to compare current asset prices, a very limited exchange rate series to judge the valuation of the currency, *very* limited series of profits and equity prices, and very little guide to what the true value of the economy was. A chart of GDP measured in dollars in the 1990s is remarkable – it shows massive growth while, supposedly, real GDP was falling each year, then it shows a massive fall before turning to steady growth when GDP was growing in real terms. The lack of precedent meant that prices were anchorless – for want of history with which to compare current prices, no one quite knew what they should be. And since there was quite extreme indeterminacy about the right price, the field was free for two extreme views to compete against each other.

Thus, while things were basically okay, and there was optimism, prices could rise and rise (where should they stop?); then in the run-up to and aftermath of the August nemesis prices could sink ridiculously low (why were these assets worth anything?).[5] Initially the first view won out and was 'proved' right (the market went up), then the second view was 'proved' right …

This may be a necessary condition for bubbles. When there is a deep price indeterminacy due to the ahistorical nature of a new asset – South Sea stocks, tulip bulbs in Amsterdam, railroad shares in the US or Russia, etc. – there is scope for great bubbles to blow up. An optimistic but untested (or barely tested) view can take root, allowing prices to sky-rocket.

Markets don't like equilibria

In the long-run I think, as I said above, that *both* opposing views on Russia will be proved to be partly right. But if that is true, why didn't the markets simply trade steadily in a gently sloping upward trajectory? That they did not, and hardly ever do, leads to a second general thought on markets and how they price things, especially things that are indeterminate.

It could well be that share prices would eventually return to, and pass, their October 1997 peak. If so, it will indicate that they were not over-valued then, at least in a sense. But why could they not have traded up and then stayed on a high plateau between 1997 and whenever this point in the future may be, trading steadily in the meantime? Or we could take the two low points of 1995–6 and 1998–9 and ask a similar question, or ask it about the whole series of ups and downs stretching from that past into the hopefully better future.

The answer seems to be that financial markets – particularly the more risky ones in which more things are more indeterminate (equity par-ticularly, and especially equity in places like Russia in 1996–8) – are very bad at staying fairly priced. If they do, they are normally volatile in a trading range for a while before breaking out one way or the other.

Put another way, there are two states that financial markets are happy with: steady upward trends (as one bullish view takes hold and more people join the bandwagon) and sharp sell-offs as investors panic. 'Stable' trading ranges include attempts at the former, plus repeated bouts of the latter. This is the only way that prices can stay close to equilibrium, and in fact no one feels at home with an equilibrium. Instead, we all prefer a good simple trend – upwards preferably, but downwards just as long as it takes to beat lots of prior optimism out of the system. Markets don't like equilibria.

LESSONS

So what have we actually learned? At least, it is pretty clear what we have not learned – that is anything about bubbles. For just as those of us most directly jarred by what went on in Russia were pondering these whys, something was bubbling up on the San Andreas Fault ... the Internet: the wave of the future, the biggest thing in the world, some-thing that is going to revolutionize the way we do business. There have to be huge amounts of money to be made out of this thing – one has to be invested, and invested early ...

Or

A technology that is all about competing margins down to nothing. While important, it is going to mean big hits for a lot of established firms as previous barriers to entry are reduced, the spread of information made almost ubiquitous and free, and inefficiencies (which most companies live off) competed down to zero. Someone will make some money for sure, but a lot more will lose …

This one has all of what Russia had: ignorance (what the hell is this thing and how can people make money out of it?), politics (everyone had to have an Internet strategy, from investors to entrepreneurs to multinationals), and emotion (the future!). Admittedly, the combination of ignorances were different this time, so the anchorlessness was different. This time the indeterminacy was not barter and obstacles to getting your hands on the wealth but lack of profits and weird valuations. What value on something that makes big losses today and will be doing nobody knows how well in five or ten years' time?

But to return to Russia, let me end by attempting a short macro explanation of what happened. Back in the mid-90s, with world markets swimming in liquidity, the Russians embarked on an aggressive stabilisation programme to bring down high inflation rates through the use of a monetary anchor. The programme combined the use of bribes (massive dollar returns for those ballsy enough to invest in rouble debt) with a rapid real appreciation – in short extremely tight monetary policy. Yeltsin's re-election was viewed as Russia's full accession to the capitalist, democratic world,[6] and monetary stabilisation was perceived as the much-heralded start of the good times in transition – growth and pro-Western progress. That benign prospect, the promise of massive returns, and the support of the international community led by the IMF added up to an irresistible bet, and the money poured in.

But the inflows were something of a stock adjustment of 'hot' short-term capital (this was to be no sustained inflow of FDI, etc.) and when the prospect of very high returns disappeared (when local interest rates fell to what were economically sustainable levels), the inducement to remain in the local debt market fell away. Capital departed following the onset of the Asian crisis. The only way to keep what remained in Russia and bring in more to finance the holes in the budget and the huge interest bill was to bribe investors with high real interest rates (essentially in dollars, assuming the currency peg held). Russia's economy, meanwhile, failed to recover as predicted, due largely to the uncompetitive exchange rate. Instead it became mired in a sea of peculiar barter and arrears, with the huge inflows of capital simply going to imports and asset price inflation, not to new production or investment. Falling oil prices combined with the highly over-valued exchange rate, extremely high real interest rates, and rampant corruption, made collecting taxes in cash as hopeless as sucking blood out of stone. But with the banking system massively short of dollars and long roubles, and the government fearful of political backlash against reforms, devaluation was not a political option, so the authorities gambled on a make-or-break course.

With the writing on the wall, everyone started bailing. Finally, the government decided to let investors take the hit rather than making the population suffer yet more through rampant inflation. Russia did the unthinkable and defaulted on its domestic debt. Russian bank debtors, given a moratorium by the government, acted like spoilt (and scared) juveniles, grabbing what they could and so stripping creditors clean. The taste it left was disgusting.

Then, while the world's investment community seethed and politicians, journalists, etc. mouthed off at the swamp that was and always would be Russia, something peculiar happened. The government under Primakov, acting like a modern-day Kutuzov, did nothing, calming an extremely fraught and depressed situation, and preventing an inflationary spiral by refusing to print large amounts of money. Even with Communists in the coalition government, there was no turning back, no renationalization, no banning of dollar purchases, etc., etc.

66Russia did the unthinkable and defaulted on its domestic debt.99

With the exchange rate now competitive and the dollars received from export revenues going that much further, the economy began to recover, as did the government's finances. Pretty soon, against the odds (in the autumn of 1998 the IMF had predicted a GDP contraction of 8 per cent for 1999 but in the end it scored +3.2 per cent), the economy was expanding rapidly, the budget was heading for balance, (reduced) debt payments were being made, etc. When oil prices started to recover, this turned into veritable excellent performance, with reserves climbing rapidly, the rouble stable and the budget running a massive surplus. Critically, there was growth in Russia's heartland as Soviet enterprises became competitive. With (rouble) costs massively reduced, they started settling in cash, producing more and investing. With Putin's election and a pro-reform, pro-Western course set, the politics and the economy had finally stabilised, just like people thought had happened in 1996.

This time there will be no bubble. Instead expect moderate, if volatile, increases in asset prices as the good news slowly seeps into a sceptical investment community. Such caution will exist for the next four or five years, until the evidence seems too compelling that Russia *really has* turned the corner. And then? Another rollercoaster? Possibly, even probably, but not quite like ours.

Notes

[1] Any views and analyses expressed in this chapter should not be assigned to a specific institution to which the author is affiliated.

[2] Boris Jordan, co-founder of Renaissance Capital Investment Bank.

[3] I remember (with some shame) discussing the industrial 'growth' of autumn 1997 at the time with two Russian colleagues and academics: we had a vote – had Russia's economy turned? We Westerners said yes, Professor Andrei Polytaev of the Russian European for Economic Policy in characteristically loud refrain, said: 'NO – rail freight traffic is not growing.' He was right of course, and the rapid growth of that same measure in early 1999 showed that the economy had turned.

[4] One anecdote of the discrepancy between Western perceptions of what was possible in Russia and the reality was an e-mail sent round by an LTCM employee in June 1998 suggesting that all the CBR had to do to get out of the meltdown was simply commence a reverse-repo auction. That in a nation on the brink of default, citizens of whose capital still, when settling the purchase of a flat, do it by placing cash in a safe deposit box with a key, in a bank, in the middle of Moscow …

[5]This undervaluation was most extreme in the case of eurobonds. After the crash bonds that had coupons of more than 10 per cent, and which the government was still current on, were trading in the teens.

[6]One ingredient traced by Kindleberger in Mania, Panics, and Crashes as a seed of most bubbles is the end of some war a good number of years before. The end of the Cold War represents that seed for our Russian bubble (and the US bubble too?).

9

CORPORATE CONSOLIDATION: RUSSIA'S LATEST LURCH TOWARDS CAPITALISM

ROLAND NASH[1]

INTRODUCTION

ONE OF THE MAJOR QUESTIONS, which resulted from Russia's seven-year experiment with an equity market, is whether equity investment in Russia is supportable even as a concept. Given the institutional environment (or lack thereof), can an equity market function? Similarly, do managers of firms, business élites or even the politicians who privatized Russia actually desire equity investment, particularly from foreigners?

Pre-crisis, for most of the economy, the answer to these questions (particularly the last) appears to have been no. The uncompetitive rouble and the structural rigidities which prevented firms profiting from changing incentives, together with a legal and regulatory infrastructure which allowed management to misallocate revenues, made profit maximization, let alone shareholder value, a very lowly maximand.

However, perhaps the most encouraging feature of the post-August 1998 investment environment is the growing evidence that this situation has changed, at least for large sections of the economy. Low equity valuations, cheap roubles, improved political stability and a shift of economic power away from the banking sector towards the real economy have catalyzed a wave of cross-industry acquisitions, mergers and share buy-backs. This in turn is changing the way in which company managers view investment and investors. It is the incentive provided by the need to raise cash, rather than federal initiatives, which is finally pushing firms to respect the market and shareholders.

This process would suggest that the Russian equity universe is splitting into two distinct groups. On one side are those firms which rely on government restructuring plans and federal initiatives to restructure. With these firms little appears to have changed, and the government seems unwilling or unable to dismantle their function as a social safety net for their employees. On the other side are those firms which are adapting to the changed incentive environment caused by the devaluation and the political stability offered by the election of President Putin. These firms are investing and acquiring assets while upgrading both management and the capital base in an attempt to maximize longer-term value. The future of the Russian economy lies with the latter group of firms.

This burgeoning trend is happening at the micro level of the economy and despite the lack of progress with macroeconomic reforms. While reform of the institutional environment remains essential if Russia is to enjoy high rates of medium-term growth, the attention being focused on macroeconomic reform is ignoring the equally important changes at the micro level. Below we focus on corporate restructuring and its possible impact. We conclude that sustainable medium-term economic growth is more likely to result from corporate restructuring finally catalyzing macro-level structural reform than vice versa.

CHANGES TO FIRMS' INCENTIVE STRUCTURE

Although the first two years after the crisis saw little progress on the structural reform front, the investment environment for much of the economy nonetheless changed markedly. The cheap rouble, high commodity prices and improved political stability combined to create a very different environment to that which faced firms before August 1998.

The exchange rate

The most obvious factor which changed was the exchange rate. The real exchange rate devalued by more than 60 per cent against the dollar between 17 August 1998, and the end of October that year. Since the end of 1998, the rouble has appreciated against the dollar in real terms by 27 per cent but still remains 35 per cent cheaper than pre-crisis levels. In producer-price terms, the rouble retains almost 40 per cent of the benefits of the devaluation, while dollar wages are still only half what they were (currently just under $100 per month). The continued impact of the devaluation is even more marked if terms-of-trade benefits from the increase in world energy prices are taken into account (see Figure 9.1).

This had a profound impact on both exporting and import-substituting firms. An average dollar received from exports is still worth 40 per cent more against average input costs compared with the pre-crisis period. Firms facing competition from imports saw their goods become 60 per cent more competitive in dollar terms by the end of 1998. This pushed many importing firms out of business and opened up a substantial market for Russian-produced goods. In the 12 months which followed August 1998, imports fell by $37 billion, opening up a potential

Figure 9.1 *The lingering impact of the exchange rate collapse (exchange rates 1997 = 100)*

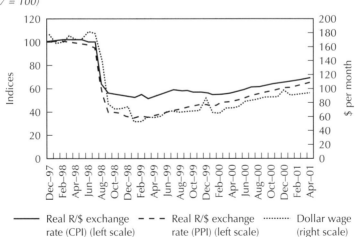

Source: Central Bank of Russia, Renaissance Capital

consumer market worth over 15 per cent of post-devaluation dollar GDP. Although consumption in real terms also fell (by 20 per cent), the price impact on demand for import-substituting firms considerably outweighed the income impact.

Increase in commodity prices

As well as the decrease in domestic costs due to devaluation, many exporters received a boost from the two-year rising trend in commodity prices. The rise and rise of oil, gas and metals prices since the end of 1998 has provided a substantial direct boost to exporters' financial situation and an indirect boost to economic growth through the multiplier impact on demand (it provided no direct impact to growth because most of the major raw materials producers were already exporting to capacity). Table 9.1 illustrates the change in profitability of Russia's major natural resource producers.

The hegemony of the real sector

The increase in profitability of the real sector together with the collapse in the banking sector has shifted economic power away from the financial sector and towards the real sector. While the two have always been linked within Russia's financial industrial groups, the dominant partners in such groups were previously the banks, with the businesses seen as entities for creating funds with which to play the financial markets.

Table 9.1 *Comparative profitability of Russian energy sector*

	Net profit ($ million)			Net profit per barrel of production		
	1998	1999	2000	1998	1999	2000
Gazprom locals	−6.213	−196	3.092	−1.75	−0.06	0.90
Gazprom ADRs	−6.213	−196	3.092	−1.75	−0.06	0.90
Surgutneftegaz	300	1.333	2.656	1.16	4.31	8.81
Lukoil	−113	916	2.927	−1.23	1.83	5.40
Yukos	−325	1.370	2.648	−1.31	4.79	7.56
PetroChina	1.845	3.261	6.673	2.38	4.21	8.72
Petrobras	378	727	5.342	1.03	1.72	11.49

Source: Company reports, Renaissance Capital

A Stalin era building is silhouetted against a winter sky as night falls in Moscow. Below, the city's Garden Ring road glows with the lights of Muscovites making their way home from work.

30 January 1997 Photo by Viktor Korotayev © Reuters 1997

Russian liberal campaigners hold a huge Russian flag in Red Square, to mark the eighth anniversary of the failure of the hardline coup against the then President Mikhail Gorbachev. They believe its failure helped to end 74 years of Communist rule and destroy the Soviet empire.

22 August 1999 Photo by Viktor Korotayev © Reuters 1999

In the centre of Moscow, a man changes the exchange rates offer for roubles. In August 1998 Russia's Central Bank suspended trade in the rouble following its steep declines against the dollar and Russians besieged banks to withdraw their life savings, hoping to swap them for dollars.

15 August 1998 Photo by Viktor Korotayev © Reuters 1998

Traders look pensive during a morning session at the main Moscow Interbank Currency Exchange (MICEX) after the Russian rouble fell further against the dollar, to 13.46.

03 September 1998 Photo by Dima Korotayev © Reuters 1998

Muscovites try to get into a bank to withdraw their savings, despite government attempts to maintain the value of the rouble. On the previous day acting Prime Minister Viktor Chernomyrdin urged Russians to think carefully before transferring savings into state savings bank Sberbank from other commercial banks.

03 September 1998 Photo by Sergei Karpukhin © Reuters 1998

Acting President Vladimir Putin (r) shakes hands with the central bank governor Viktor Gerashchenko during a meeting in the Kremlin to discuss the state of the country's economy.

03 January 2000 Photo by ITAR-TASS © Reuters 2000

The Astra oil drilling platform in the Russian sector of the Caspian sea, 70kms from the city of Astrakhan. Russia recently announced it had become the third country to find oil in the inland.

23 March 2000 © Reuters 2000

Russian President Vladimir Putin (l) standing with the first Russian President Boris Yeltsin during his inauguration ceremony in the Kremlin. Putin vowed to unite the nation, repay people's trust and take care of the country he inherited from Yeltsin in Russia's first democratic handover of power.

07 May 2000 Photo by ITAR-TASS © Reuters 2000

"Oligarchs no longer focus on acquiring assets through the political clout of their banks in the financial markets but through mergers and takeovers via their businesses."

Since the crisis and the collapse in Russia's financial markets, the businesses have grown to become the profit centres, with the banks seen simply as a means of handling excess revenues.

This relative increase in the importance of the real sector has been one of the major causes of the new focus on business building and consolidation. Oligarchs no longer focus on acquiring assets through the political clout of their banks in the financial markets but through mergers and takeovers via their businesses. Moreover, the aim of acquiring assets is no longer to strip value and pass it out through the banking arm but to build out and increase revenue streams.

The shrinkage in non-payments

Non-monetary forms of payment dominated commercial transactions before the crisis. According to some estimates, more than 70 per cent of transactions within industry took place in some form of non-payment,[2] and this number was substantially higher in certain sectors, such as the utilities. Subsidization of the real, non-energy sector of the economy by the utilities and natural resource sector was enormous – estimates range up to 10 per cent of GDP in explicit subsidies and a further 10 per cent in implicit subsidies.[3] This itself implies a massive misallocation of resources, even seven years after privatisation and price liberalization were supposed to have permitted the market to allocate resources more efficiently. Evidently, non-payments substantially undermined that potentially beneficial process.

While much has been written on the underlying reasons for Russia's predilection towards non-payments, the basic cause was a combination of firms not generating sufficient return on capital given the risk environment, together with absence of the institutional environment needed to enforce a hard budget constraint. While the institutional environment has not improved, the devaluation has meant that it is no longer cost-effective to transact in non-payments. Since August 1998, non-payments have virtually disappeared. Even within the utilities sector, cash collection rates are approaching 100 per cent. This has removed a substantial cost to the economy and abolished a major factor hamstringing enterprises.

Increased political stability

The improvement in the overall macroeconomic environment caused by the crisis was partially overshadowed during 1999 by continuing political uncertainty. Russia suffered three prime ministers during 1999, reflecting underlying political instability caused primarily by an absence of centralized authority together with weak political institutions, which were unable to maintain a separation between the public and private spheres. Under these conditions business and political élites were able to move freely between the two spheres and exploit their positions in both. Looming over this chaos was the uncertainty surrounding parliamentary and presidential elections scheduled for December 1999 and June–July 2000 respectively. With enormous uncertainty surrounding the type of regime which would emerge from the elections, horizons were limited and the environment favoured continuation of the business practices of the mid-90s, despite the improvement in economic conditions resulting from the crisis.

The surprisingly positive outcome of the parliamentary elections (the Russian Trading System (RTS) jumped by 17 per cent the day the results became known) and the election of Vladimir Putin to replace the ailing Boris Yeltsin as president established substantially greater political certainty. The successful implementation of policies designed to increase centralized authority since Mr Putin's election has served to establish a sense of order in politics. While Russia may not yet enjoy strong political institutions, the country does at least have the rule of Putin, if not yet the rule of law. As a result of the substantial decrease in political uncertainty, businesses are more able to think longer term when planning how to take advantage of the changed incentives and improved business environment resulting from the crisis.

CHANGING OWNERSHIP STRUCTURE

Aside from the altered economic environment, there has been substantial change in the ownership structure of Russian firms. Managers of large sections of industry have been consolidating their position within firms and increasing their stake towards a super-majority 75 per cent +1 share holding. Once in possession of a super-majority stake, companies are immune to the actions of a blocking minority and can essentially implement whichever policies they choose.

Control of assets is all-important in a weak and confused institutional environment which is not able to provide protection for assets. Pre-crisis, management of assets was enough, since management was interested in the misdirection of revenue streams from the assets rather than in the assets themselves. The change in the economic environment described above has meant that owning assets is now important because asset value, rather than mere revenue streams, has significance. Hence the struggle to gain 75 per cent + 1 share stakes.

Moreover, the dynamic runs both ways. The ownership of 75 per cent + 1 share in a company provides both the security and the incentive to manage those assets more sensibly and therefore profitably. Most importantly from a shareholder perspective, it also provides the incentive to encourage the share price upwards. This is the major reason why we are excited, from an equity perspective, about the consolidation process.

Figure 9.2 shows the change in profitability at Yukos relative to Lukoil. As it illustrates, Yukos began outperforming Lukoil on profitability per barrel exactly at the time that its management gained a 75 per cent super-majority. Misdirecting revenues became less important than increasing asset value once management had secured its 75 per cent stake. Similarly, management were not afraid of showing profits once they had complete control over the company.

Figure 9.2 *Lukoil vs Yukos profitability per barrel*

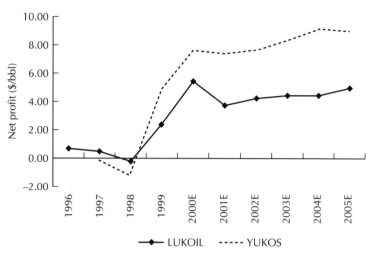

Source: Renaissance Capital

EVIDENCE OF A CHANGE IN BUSINESS ATTITUDES SINCE AUGUST 1998

The changes in the investment environment and the changes in ownership structure outlined above have had a major impact on the managers' attitude to doing business in Russia. These changes include the reinvestment of revenues to accumulate assets in Russia, purchase of assets in the 'near abroad', particularly the Commonwealth of Independent States (CIS) and Eastern Europe, investment into own companies and the issuance of corporate debt. The changes are described below.

Transfer of share ownership back to Russia

In broad terms, the process of privatisation in Russia between 1992 and the beginning of 2001 can be split into four phases.

■ *Phase 1.* Between 1992 and 1995 voucher privatisation and the first, more or less, public auctions were conducted. This process, designed by Anatoly Chubais, resulted in the privatisation of much of Russian industry, albeit with substantial state influence remaining.

■ *Phase 2*. Between 1994 and 1997, there was an initial wave of consolidation of holdings within firms, both through the purchase of shares acquired by workers and management during voucher privatisation, and through the direct purchase of larger packets of shares at auctions (most famously during the shares-for-loans debacle ahead of the 1996 presidential elections). Much of this second wave was organized by the banking sector, which was then flush with cash following profits made during the high inflation years of 1992–4, and the returns generated from the monstrously high interest rates on government debt in 1995–6. The Russian oligarchy emerged during this second wave of privatisation.

■ *Phase 3*. The third wave involved the transfer of large blocks of shares abroad into the hands of foreigners. It began in 1994 but only really took off in earnest after the 1996 presidential election when it became clear that Russia was not about to turn its back on private ownership. This wave of international money hit a relatively illiquid equity market and created the bubble that burst at the end of 1997. During the bubble's expansion, shares in second, third and fourth-tier firms moved abroad as foreign portfolio money flowed into Russia, incidentally financing Russian capital moving abroad.

■ *Phase 4*. The most recent stage of ownership evolution has been the reversal of the trend towards foreign ownership. Since the beginning of 1999, Russian companies have been actively buying back the shares sold abroad in 1996–8. Much of the investment banking and brokerage business of 1999 and 2000 has consisted of organizing buy-backs of share packets from foreign holders on behalf of domestic firms. With shares at less than one-third of their 1997 value, owners have a real incentive to buy back shares they sold abroad for a premium three years ago. This two-year process has seen a considerable consolidation of ownership within Russian firms, driven fundamentally by a turnaround in profitability since the devaluation. While, again, this trend is difficult to isolate within the balance of payments figures, it is interesting to note that traditional forms of capital flight have declined, even though the flow of capital abroad is still high. Much of the capital flight in 2000 may be explained by the flow of Russian capital abroad to pay for the repurchase of shares sold in 1997.

Joining the dots across Eastern Europe

Another noticeable trend since Russia's major exporting companies began to generate significant excess revenues has been the accumulation of assets in CIS countries and former Soviet satellite countries in Eastern Europe. It would appear that Russian companies are utilizing a substantial portion of the revenues taken abroad as capital flight to purchase assets in these countries. In many cases, the companies being bought were earlier separated from their Russian mother-companies in the breakdown of the Comecon bloc. Companies like Gazprom and Lukoil are using their excess revenues to rebuild business empires which they lost during the past decade. The strategy of reuniting companies with which historic links exist makes much sense for the managers of Russian companies. While they have little comparative advantage competing in Western markets, they have a much stronger understanding of the business model that exists in Eastern Europe and the CIS.

> **❝The strategy of reuniting companies with which historic links exist makes much sense for the managers of Russian companies.❞**

Investment trends

The most positive piece of macroeconomic news during 2000 was the turnaround in domestic investment. After falling by 80 per cent between 1992 and 1998, investment grew by 17 per cent in 2000. Given the small base number, even this 17 per cent increase leaves absolute investment low, and after the capital depreciation of the past decade, Russia needs to see growth rates of this order for several more years before absolute improvement in the overall capital base will become noticeable.

Nevertheless, the increase in investment is encouraging. Moreover, the investment has been made in those firms and those sectors that have proved most successful since the devaluation. Table 9.2 shows the capital investment of several of the oil majors since 1997 and would indicate that these firms at least are actively improving their capital base.

Table 9.2 *Oil sector investment ($m)*

	1997	1998	1999	2000E	2001E	2002E
Gazprom	7135	3140	4064	4196	4927	4927
Lukoil	1900	1712	1250	2143	2024	2294
Surgutneftegaz	980	600	530	1131	1316	1862
Yukos	n.a.	169	176	551	1030	1760
Sibneft	562	185	120	321	665	693
Tatneft	608	790	319	470	573	621
Total	**10578**	**5805**	**6140**	**8343**	**9963**	**11536**

Source: Companies, Renaissance Capital

Consolidation within and across industries

Another clear trend that emerged in 2000 was towards consolidation of a greater portion of industry into a smaller number of hands. President Vladimir Putin has been actively pushing business out of politics, but has resolutely left the oligarchs to their own devices in the economy. Given negative real interest rates and the cheap valuation of many companies, this *laissez faire* approach has sparked a trend towards inter- and intra-industry consolidation.

The following are just some of the headline consolidations that are taking place across Russia. The list of consolidations, which is by no means comprehensive, includes:

■ *The aluminium industry.* Over the past 18 months, the aluminium industry has changed from being comprised of a large number of smaller smelters to being consolidated into two huge conglomerates, Russian Aluminium (RusAl) and Siberian-Urals Aluminium (SUAL). RusAl is linked to Roman Abramovich and, through him, to the oil company Sibneft. RusAL includes the Bratsk and Krasnoyarsk aluminium plants and the Siberian Aluminium company. SUAL is owned by US-based Renova and Access Industries, which also owns 50 per cent of Tyumen Oil Company (TNK). SUAL controls the Urals, Irkutsk, Kandulagsha and Bogaslovsk aluminium plants. While both conglomerates are keen to emphasize their independence from other industries, it is clear that they both have close links to the oil sector. More recently, the aluminium sector has been expanding into downstream production, specifically the purchase by Siberian Aluminium of the car manufacturing company GAZ.

- *Gazprom.* Sibur, a company with close links to Gazprom, has been rapidly buying up oil product-linked companies across Russia, the CIS and Eastern Europe – everything from the Omsk Tyre Plant to Hungarian chemical producer BorsodChem. Exactly how many acquisitions have been made is unclear, but Sibur, and by extension Gazprom, now has holdings across a large number of Russian industries.

- *Tatneft.* Tatneft is the jewel in the crown of the economy of the Republic of Tatarstan. The company has been accumulating assets at the regional level in the same way as more geographically diversified energy companies have been doing at the national level. Tatneft's largest acquisition to date has been the enormous Nizhnekamsk Tyre Plant, a company that was on the verge of bankruptcy before being injected with Tatneft's oil money. Whereas Tatneft previously supported the Tatar economy through financing non-payments and direct subsidization of the regional government, the oil company now has managerial control over the companies that it supports.

- *Severstal.* Severstal steel plant has been diversifying to move into downstream production. Over the past 12 months the company has purchased ZMZ (Zavolzhsk Motor Plant), UAZ (Ulyanovsk Automotive Plant) and the Kolomensk Machinery Plant, as well as making a number of smaller acquisitions.

- *Baltika Brewery.* The successful St Petersburg-based beer brewer has been busy increasing its capacity by purchasing beer factories across Russia. Over the past 12 months, Baltika has purchased roughly three breweries.

- *Wimm-Bill-Dann.* The singularly successful Russian food producer, has been purchasing breweries, with an eye towards producing its own beer brand. In the past two years, the company has taken over more than ten breweries throughout Russia. Similarly, it has been focusing on purchasing domestic dairies to increase its own production.

■ *The pulp and paper industry*. As with the aluminium industry, the pulp and paper industry until recently consisted of a large number of small producers, and is rapidly consolidating into two or three large groupings.

■ *The oil industry*. TNK and Lukoil are both rapidly expanding their upstream and downstream businesses. TNK spent $1.1 billion to purchase the oil producer Onako, while Lukoil bought KomiTEK and is trying to increase its ownership of refineries in Eastern Europe and the CIS.

The logic behind this consolidation process is clear. Equity valuations are, by any measure, very low. As Figure 9.3 suggests, Russian equity is cheap relative to its international peers. Russian equity is very cheap even relative to the country's sovereign debt spreads, suggesting that there is a large risk premium being added to Russian companies.

This large risk premium is mainly a result of fears over corporate governance. A series of shareholders' rights violations, coupled with memories of the August 1998 crisis, have left most investors worried that they have no control over funds invested in Russian companies. Despite the very low valuations, therefore, there is a reluctance to invest.

Figure 9.3 *Payment for corporate governance: market PEs vs sovereign spreads*

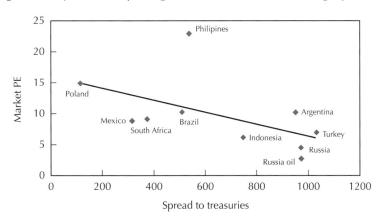

Source: Renaissance Capital

However, the Russian business élite does not face the same risk profile, as they are considerably more able to monitor the actions of management. In many cases, consolidation has resulted in super-majority ownership (75 per cent + 1 share), providing complete control over management. With cash earning 0 per cent in real terms, and with company valuations at current low levels because of risks not faced by those who can gain a majority stake, it is not surprising that mergers, acquisitions and takeovers are multiplying in the current economic environment.

IMPLICATIONS OF FIRM-LEVEL REFORM

The shift in the incentive environment facing Russian firms and the resulting change in business practices have several implications for Russia's equity market. Those stocks which are adapting to the changed incentive environment and are investing, restructuring and acquiring assets are likely to benefit. Those stocks which rely on federal-level reforms and provide management with little incentive to alter behaviour are unlikely to adapt and will therefore suffer as the rouble becomes less competitive.

- *Firm-level restructuring is compensating for slow progress on federal reforms.* Historically, attention has been focused on the progress (or lack thereof) of reforms as implemented at the federal level. Following the August 1998 financial crisis, investors have viewed promises of reform implementation with deep scepticism, and the burden of proof has been with Russia. As equity-market valuations have been determined by fund flows into Russia, investing has been simply a function of guessing when money would be allocated to Russia, which was itself a function of headline news over reform implementation (at least from a purely Russian perspective). If, however, the main trend of restructuring has been happening at the firm level rather than the federal level, then the equity market is focusing on the wrong indicator. Just as the level of inflation and the stability of the rouble in 1996–8 disguised the dismal profitability and non-payments crushing industry, so the fixation with federal reforms in 1999 and 2000 has missed the restructuring taking place at the enterprise level.

- *Choice of company has become important.* Restructuring is not occurring universally. While a significant portion of industry is reacting to the change in the incentive environment facing firms, there remain large sections of industry which are content to enjoy the increased profitability without altering their actions. There is little incentive to restructure and reform for firms with majority government stakes, and which are acting as the government's substitute social safety net. Indeed, given the incentive environment imposed by the federal government, some of Russia's most important firms cannot restructure radically even if management so desired. Within the parameters set by the government, management behaviour is little changed from before the crisis.

- *Corporate governance remains singularly important.* The absence of a secure institutional framework to protect minority shareholders means that the alignment of interests between management and shareholders must be a decisive factor in determining asset allocation. The whole chain of minority shareholder rights violations in the second half of 2000 illustrates again that investors cannot rely on the law to protect their interests. Consequently it is necessary to choose investment vehicles that align the interests of minority shareholders with those of company management, thereby circumventing the principal-agent problem of a small shareholder. The way to do this is either to choose firms which need the services of the market (although this runs the danger of being only a temporary arrangement) or to choose those firms which have no need to dilute shareholders any further because one block already own a super-majority stake (more than 75 per cent + 1 share).

Reduced transparency

66 The most blatant example of difficulties due to consolidation is at Gazprom, Russia's gas monopoly. 99

The flip-side of the increased investment and corporate restructuring is the threat of reduced transparency as a result of consolidation. Cross-subsidization is rife throughout Russian industry. This is partly a result of political necessity, with large sections of Russian industry kept afloat through cross-subsidization from the energy sector due to a combination of price fixing and poor enforcement of contract law. It is equally a result of a desire to deliberately increase confusion in order to prevent a detailed analysis by tax inspectors and creditors.

The creation of large, cross-industry conglomerates increases the scope for further cross-subsidization and opaqueness. The most blatant example of difficulties due to consolidation is at Gazprom, Russia's gas monopoly. Partly because of the debts owed to it, and partly because of the excess cash funds it generates, Gazprom has been one of the major acquirers of companies over the past two years. These companies have ranged from Perm GPZ, a petrochemical plant, to Omski tyre factory. Many of the firms acquired have little to do with Gazprom's core competence and if improved through acquisition have only been so because of their even more abysmal starting point.

Growing influence of a small group of individuals

A second more insidious trend has been the dynamic by which larger business interests increase their political influence and are thereby able to accelerate accumulation of further assets. While President Putin has had considerable success at pushing business out of federal politics, economic power retains substantial influence. Although the oligarchs are no longer able to dictate federal policy through playing politics (witness the downfall of Boris Berezovsky and Vladimir Gusinsky), economic interests remain influential within the economic sphere of politics. The failure of the Putin administration at implementing reform when faced with opposition from entrenched economic interest groups is illustrative – while Mr Putin has had considerable success in implementing tax reform, budget reform and trade reform, he has made virtually no progress in restructuring the banking sector, the utilities sector or the natural monopolies (particularly Gazprom and the Railways Ministry).

The consolidation of the 'commanding heights' of Russian industry within the hands of a relatively small number of individuals or groups does not bode well for breaking the dominance of economic interests over politics. The two groups which have fared best under Putin are

Alfa Group and the amorphous grouping around the tycoon Roman Abramovich. It is no coincidence that these two interest groups are the least active in openly playing federal politics – neither controls important media interests. However, they have both managed to accumulate a number of important industrial assets under Mr Putin. Roman Abramovich has created a virtual monopoly over the aluminium industry, and has more recently turned his attention towards the car industry, while Alfa Group has swallowed Onako, an oil firm. If industry becomes more consolidated, then it is virtually inevitable that the resulting groups will extend their influence over politics.

CONCLUSION

Before the August 1998 devaluation, the incentive environment facing firms was simple, if somewhat warped. The overpriced rouble and the economic and political turmoil meant that the majority of Russian industry was either not capable of generating the returns to justify capital employed or was simply not profitable. Moreover, the absence of any meaningful hard-budget constraint or the institutional environment to enforce contract law meant that resources could not be redeployed. Under these circumstances, firms were incentivized to renege on costs (particularly taxes, energy and wages) and to divert revenues abroad as rapidly as possible, while going bankrupt to the right people in order to adopt assets again under a new guise. Under such circumstances, equity investors and minority stakeholders were simply an inconvenience. Equity investment in the sense of oversight and company valuation simply had no impact on firm behaviour.

In the two-and-a-half years since devaluation, the incentive environment has completely changed. The cheap rouble has meant that firms can make substantial profits while paying costs more or less in full. The improvement in political stability since the election of President Putin has greatly improved the risk environment, justifying investment given increased profitability. It would be remarkably strange if the shift in incentives did not have an impact on firms' behaviour. As it is, there is growing evidence that firms are becoming considerably more market orientated and focused on making a return on assets. Investment has increased dramatically, firms are being taken over, management is changing, and shares are being repurchased from foreign holders.

This change in firm behaviour and the restructuring it represents has important consequences for the equity market. At the most basic level, it now means that an equity market has a function in Russia. Firms are profitable, meaning that shareholders have at least a theoretical hope of a return, while company management is becoming more aware that acting in the interests of the market has a positive benefit for them. Enterprise restructuring, while having obvious macroeconomic benefits, is fundamentally firm-specific. This makes it of paramount importance to choose those firms which are reacting to the changed incentive environment. Finally, within the subset of firms that are actively restructuring, it is equally important to choose those which most closely align the incentives of management with the incentives of small shareholders.

Notes

[1] Any views and analyses expressed in this chapter should not be assigned to a specific institution to which the author is affiliated.

[2] For ease of notation, non-payment is used to cover a whole range of non-monetary forms of payment, including barter, avoidance and refusal to pay.

[3] See World Bank report 'Give growth and macro stability in Russia a chance: harden budgets by dismantling nonpayments', Brian Pinto *et al.*, 2000.

10

DEBT SERVICING, RUSSIAN STYLE

KASPER BARTHOLDY[1]

INTRODUCTION

THE RUSSIAN GOVERNMENT IS WELL on the way towards regaining access to international bond markets. President Vladimir Putin commands sufficient political power at home to pursue serious market-friendly economic reform if he so desires. On the back of the past year's political change and sky-rocketing prices for Russian oil and gas exports, spreads on Russian eurobonds have lost their 'stratospheric' status and are now just 'very high'. Russia's international credit ratings are recovering. It is in the hands of Putin and his government to ensure a further rapid improvement in Russia's creditworthiness and a fall in spreads on sovereign eurobonds.

At this stage, spreads on Russian debt remain high mainly because of residual doubts in the market about the government's 'willingness to pay'. After having defaulted on most of its obligations over the past few years, the government has yet to offer a clear promise that all residual obligations will now be serviced on current terms. The people who ruled Russia in 1998 clearly did not feel constrained by a sense of 'moral obligation' to pay their debts. The current government has yet to convince the markets that it has genuinely broken with past practices and has adopted a stringent and transparent set of principles for debt service. The evolution of these principles will, over the next few years, arguably be as important an influence on Russian debt yields as will, for example, the government's progress on structural reform.

Although the central bank is accumulating foreign exchange reserves at a rapid pace, the finance ministry continues to insist in public statements that it may need further major debt forgiveness from foreign creditor governments. These creditor governments have already swallowed the impact of several rounds of Russian debt restructuring over the past decade.

The Russian government also remains non-committal towards the servicing of some of its debt to private creditors, notably the so-called MinFin series IV and V. These are securities that represent previously restructured hard currency obligations of the Soviet foreign trade bank. The government has not, at this stage, clearly ruled out further restructuring of these securities, although it is increasingly emphasizing that any such restructuring would be market-based.

The main international ratings agencies have raised Russia's eurobonds ratings substantially since the time of the GKO defaults in 1998. But they will find it hard to upgrade Russian sovereign ratings more than one or two notches until the government clarifies its debt servicing principles. In order to pave the way for more dramatic credit upgrades, the government will have to convey to the world that it is prepared to service its debt as a matter of principle, and not just because oil prices are strong or because debt servicing happens to be convenient and easy at the present time. As the overview below will show, the government seems to be edging towards adopting the view that debt should be paid as a matter of principle, but it still has some work to do to convey this message convincingly to the market. The rating agencies and the markets will also look for clearer evidence that the Russian central bank and the government will not in the future waste scarce FX reserves in an effort to keep the rouble/dollar exchange rate stable in the face of heavy depreciation pressure (as they did in 1998 when the wish to defend an unrealistic exchange rate was among the key triggers of the government's debt service defaults).

WHY DOES ANY GOVERNMENT REPAY ITS DEBT?

Why do governments elsewhere in the world bother to pay their debt? Governments are rarely taken to court, and it is difficult for debtors to impound the assets of debtor governments. It is arguably optimal for governments to borrow as much as possible and then forget about the obligation to repay. That is essentially what the Russian government did in 1997–8. Why is this not common behaviour?

> **Creditworthiness makes it easier for domestic enterprises and banks to entice foreign financing for new production plants and equipment.**

An important reason for governments to service their debt, over and beyond issues of 'pride and morals', is that creditworthiness yields economic benefits. Continued access to credit offers a borrower, be it a government or an enterprise, the ability to smooth out the effect of shocks and to overcome liquidity bottlenecks. Access to trade finance, in particular, plays a key role in the development of the export and import sectors. Creditworthiness makes it easier for domestic enterprises and banks to entice foreign financing for new production plants and equipment. Uninterrupted debt service by a country's rulers helps signal to potential investors (foreign as well as domestic) that the government takes its other promises seriously. This helps strengthen the sense among investors that they can participate as owners of production facilities in the debtor country without being faced with excessive risk of expropriation or of arbitrary government rulings against them. The actions of the Russian government in 1998–9 sent the opposite signal.

IS IT POSSIBLE TO MAKE SENSE OF THE RUSSIAN DEBT SERVICE BEHAVIOUR IN 1998–9?

Most analysts would accept that the Kirienko government was forced to devalue the rouble in August 1998 (and most would argue that it should have done so much earlier than it did). Some would even argue that the government had no choice but to default on its rouble debt in August 1998. But even the greatest Russia apologists would find it hard to argue that the government was forced to default on its Paris Club obligations in the autumn of 1998, MinFin IIIs in May 1999, Prins in December 1998, and IANs in June 1999 ('Prins' and 'IANs' were labels used to denote different categories of London Club debt). It is harder still to argue that the government was forced by financial constraints to prevent Russia's corporate sector from servicing its debt to foreigners, as it did in 1998.

One of the most intriguing aspects of the Russian debt service behaviour in 1998–9 was that the government opted to continue to service its sovereign eurobond liabilities and parts of its debt to foreign governments at a time when it had defaulted on almost all of its other debt. Ignoring for the moment any moral considerations (as indeed the government seemed to do at the time), it is by no means clear that this 'continued partial debt servicing' was rational. After defaulting on virtually all other obligations, the reputational extra cost associated with default on eurobonds would arguably have been small. The massive eurobond spreads prevailing at the end of 1998 show that the market at the time expected the government to default on the eurobonds. An actual default would only have satisfied the market's expectations. So why didn't the government default on the eurobonds?

The government has argued that it was indeed, in 1998–9, guided by a morally defensible code, which dictated uninterrupted debt service for 'new Russian debt' and restructuring for 'old Soviet debt'. This code involved continued servicing of the eurobonds.

■ The term 'Soviet debt' was used intensively by the government in 1998 and 1999 to refer to debt that was contracted before 1 January 1992. The concept included all of the debt that was rescheduled in the mid-1990s under the auspices of the London Club and the Paris Club. It also included three of the five series of MinFin bonds that remained outstanding at the end of 1998.

■ The government used the term 'new Russian debt' to include all those FX-denominated liabilities which the Russian Federation has contracted since 1992. This included all of the government's eurobond liabilities as well as some FX-denominated debt to foreign governments and all of the government's debt to multilateral institutions (notably the IMF and the World Bank). It also included (according to the government's own interpretation) two of the five outstanding series of MinFin bonds.

Coarsely speaking, the argument that underlies the government's distinction between Soviet and Russian debt runs along the following lines. The world should understand that the government made a mistake in 1991–2, when it assumed responsibility for the Soviet Union's foreign debt. This was an undertaking which the country could ill afford. The responsibility for this debt really rests with the old Communist rulers of the Soviet Union and not with the new Russian Federation. The world at large should, therefore, allow the government to shirk responsibility for at least a part of this debt. A poor debt servicing record for this debt should not undermine the world's view of the overall creditworthiness of the Russian government which has maintained an uncompromising commitment to the servicing of all 'its own' debt.

This argument is, however, somewhat hollow. All of the local currency debt, on which the government defaulted in 1998, was 'new Russian debt'. It had all been issued long after the new Russian Federation became an independent entity. Even the rescheduled 'Soviet' debt arguably became 'new Russian' obligations as far back as the early 1990s when the Russian Federation offered to the other former Soviet republics that it would assume responsibility for all the Soviet Union's debt. This offer was confirmed in the mid-1990s when the Russian Federation agreed with its foreign creditors to have its debt restructured under the purview of the London Club and the Paris Club.

The government's dominant decision criterion seems instead to have been to default on as wide an array of liabilities as possible, subject to an overriding wish to stay current on eurobonds. The latter wish implied continued servicing of all debt that was linked to eurobonds through 'cross-acceleration clauses'. Such cross-acceleration clauses were included in the prospectuses for all the sovereign Russian eurobonds that were outstanding at the time. These clauses dictated that if the government were to default on one of its eurobonds, then the holders of any other sovereign eurobonds would have the right immediately to put their entire claim to the government at par. In fact the phrasing of the cross-acceleration clauses was even broader than that. If the government were to default on any FX-denominated liability (not just eurobonds) that had not explicitly been identified as 'excluded debt', then holders of any sovereign eurobond had the right to present the government with a claim for 'accelerated payment'. In order to avoid such accelerated payment claims on eurobonds, the government continued to service all FX-denominated debt that was not identified as 'excluded debt'.

Meanwhile, the government defaulted on virtually all categories of 'excluded' FX debt. In addition, of course, it defaulted pretty comprehensively on its local currency debt. The 'excluded' FX debt comprised all sovereign FX-denominated debt that originated before the end of 1991. The bulk of this had been restructured in the mid-1990s in negotiated deals with the London Club and the Paris Club.

The government's decision to continue debt service payments on its 'Russian' FX debt required little sacrifice. The debt that the government continued to service in 1999 represented a minor proportion of the government's overall debt stock. The government knew that its debt to the IMF and the World Bank could not be restructured for institutional reasons (the IMF and the World Bank offer debt restructuring only to the poorest countries in the world). 'New Russian debt' represented only 10 per cent of the government's total liabilities to other debtors than the IMF and the World Bank. The categories of debt on which the government eventually defaulted represented more than 80 per cent of its total outstanding obligations in mid-1998.

These considerations still leave open the question that was raised above: why was it so important for the government to stay current on the eurobonds? There is no easy answer to this. But a possible explanation is that the government genuinely feared the legal consequences of eurobond default. The legal consequences of defaulting on other debt did not seem correspondingly threatening.

To understand this argument, it is important to recognize that the eurobonds were claims on the Russian sovereign and were subject to English law. The GKOs and MinFins, on the other hand, were subject only to Russian law. The London Club debt instruments (the IANs and

Prins) were governed by English law but represented claims 'only' on the (effectively bankrupt) foreign trade bank, rather than claims on the sovereign. For these reasons, eurobond holders would probably have found it easier to push through a legal claim for compensation than would the holders of IANs, Prins, GKOs or MinFins (although there have been attempts by MinFin holders to pursue their claims through the Russian court system).

On this basis the government may well have concluded that the likely cost of default on eurobonds would have outweighed the potential benefit. While the possible costs were never easy to gauge, the government probably thought lawsuits by eurobond holders could have led to widespread seizure of government assets abroad. Meanwhile, the potential benefits of default were limited by the fact that only a modest stock of sovereign eurobonds was outstanding in late 1998. This restricted the cashflow savings that could have been extracted from a comprehensive eurobond default.

Many analysts have argued that the decision to continue to service the eurobonds was also based on the government's expectation that it would, in the absence of default, a few years later be able to issue new eurobonds. But it is by no means obvious that continued eurobond service would bring cashflow advantages to the government within a relevant time frame. Although the interest and principal payments on eurobonds were small in 1998–9, it was clear in late 1998 that the government would not, for many years, be able to raise sufficient FX from new eurobond issuance to outweigh the outflows that derived from having to continue to service the outstanding eurobonds.

66the potential benefits of default were limited by the fact that only a modest stock of sovereign eurobonds was outstanding in late 1998.99

There are other possible explanations for the government's decision to service the eurobonds. One is that the key ministers may have been sufficiently clairvoyant to recognize that they would need the sovereign eurobonds to remain untarnished (as an asset class) in order to be able to use the eurobond concept as a tool in subsequent negotiations with the London Club. We now know that the government's offer of an upgrade of London Club debt to eurobond status eventually helped persuade the London Club creditors in early 2000 to accept a large reduction in their nominal claim on the Russian government.

It is also possible that the decision to continue servicing of eurobonds was an accidental result of a very messy process of decision making within the Russian government rather than a component of a carefully thought-out strategy. Other debt-service decisions made by the government in 1998–9 certainly appeared deeply irrational from the outset, indicating that careful planning and consideration was not an important driver of the decisions. The most startling example was the government's decision to default comprehensively on its rouble-denominated T-bill debt in August 1998. This decision effectively killed the domestic banking system and destroyed the government's ability to borrow for a protracted period thereafter. This was a heavy price to pay for a very limited gain. The gain was small because the impact of the T-bill default on the government's indebtedness was dwarfed by the impact later in 1998 of sharp currency depreciation and high inflation. It is pretty clear that the government would have done much better for itself (and for the country) by avoiding default on the rouble debt, given that the real value of the debt was wiped out anyway by the decision (also taken by the government and the central bank in August 1998) to let the currency slide.

LINGERING DOUBTS ABOUT THE 'WILLINGNESS TO PAY'

Whatever the real motives of the government may have been, its decision to embark on 'selective default' in 1998–9 remains an important influence on creditor considerations now. During debt restructuring talks with the Russian government in 1999–2000, the London Club creditors went out of their way to create legal safeguards against a repeat of the 1998 experience. They wanted to ensure that the government would, in the future, have no repeat opportunity to default selectively on London Club debt. The eventual London Club debt restructuring (in the third quarter of 2000) resulted in the creation of two eurobonds, the so-called '10s and '30s. The prospectuses for the new bonds ensure that if the government were to default on the '10s or the '30s, holders of other eurobonds would be legally entitled to put their claim to the government at par. It is still imaginable that the government could persuade these holders of other eurobonds to abstain from making use of their cross-acceleration rights (in case of a default on '10s and '30s). But although another round of selective default is not entirely impossible, the language of the prospectuses for the '10s and '30s at least goes a long way towards reducing the risk.

The appearance of opportunism (and/or chaos) in the Russian debt decisions in 1998–9 continues to influence Russian sovereign credit spreads. A substantial further favourable leap in Russia's credit standing over the next few years will require the government to signal clearly to international bond markets that a true regime shift has taken place and that the government's debt service is guided by a genuine sense of obligation to pay back debt.

RECENT SIGNS OF A MORE RESPECTABLE RUSSIAN DEBT SERVICE APPROACH

Some of President Putin's broad policy statements seem to indicate a determination to adopt a more respectable approach to debt servicing. The very fact that the government is seeking to normalize the vast bulk of its creditor relations is also a promising sign. The most recent example is the government's new restructuring agreement with the holders of the so-called foreign trade obligations (a type of Soviet-era debt that has never previously been restructured). An even more important example was Putin's decision in early 2001 to overrule his finance ministry and dictate that Russia's debt to the Paris Club should be serviced in accordance with current contractual terms, at least until the government and the creditors have agreed on new payment terms. The eurobond market should welcome these efforts by the government in general and by the president in particular. The market should also welcome Putin's emphasis on fiscal prudence and his declaration that inflation is among the government's main enemies.

It would arguably be in the government's best interest to build on this foundation and declare that Russia is now a country that can stand on its own two feet, a country that has no need for further debt restructuring from either the Paris Club or other creditors. The central bank's stock of foreign currency reserves is sufficiently comfortable to allow the government to make such a declaration with some comfort. The absence of such a declaration sends the uncomfortable signal to the market that the government and the central bank would be less than fully prepared to tighten fiscal and monetary policy and let the exchange rate adapt if oil prices were to fall. It is in the interest of the government to help eradicate this perception.

In the absence of such a roadmap, the government's credit standing would continue to be dented by creditor doubt about broad governmental debt service intentions and from uncertainty among private-sector creditors about the extent to which Paris Club creditors might at some point, as a condition for future 'comprehensive' restructuring arrangements, insist that the government also seeks further restructuring of its liabilities to creditors in the private sector.

Note

[1] Any views and analyses expressed in this chapter should not be assigned to a specific institution to which the author is affiliated

PART IV

Out of the wilderness

11

THE CHALLENGE OF ECONOMIC POLICY, INVESTMENTS AND GROWTH

YEVGENY GAVRILENKOV AND NICLAS SUNDSTRÖM[1]

THE SECOND PHASE OF RUSSIA'S REVOLUTION

SEVERAL INFLUENTIAL STUDIES HAVE SEEN the period 2000–1 as a rejuvenated second, and different, phase of major economic reform in Russia, taking the launch of radical economic reform in 1992 as the first phase.[2] One inherent challenge in this second phase of Russian reforms is the pursuit of economic policies – mainly structural and institutional – which foster improvement of the investment climate, providing incentives and a framework conducive to private-sector productivity growth, investment and development.[3]

Here we attempt to reflect on this issue from different perspectives. The near-term key economic policy initiatives, which are likely to impact on investment trends, are identified and discussed, along with the pattern and behaviour of investment flows. We will argue that investment patterns – both official and anecdotal – have already begun to recognize the importance of the critical mass of mainly structural and institutional reforms now being pursued. At the same time, continuation of this positive trend will require tangible progress in a selected number of policy areas, highlighting the role of sequencing coalition

building for important reforms as well as choosing a realistic benchmark to be used when assessing Russian reform progress at this stage.

The current rejuvenated push for structural and economic reforms is
taking place amid lingering outside concerns over Russian affairs. Some
of these concerns are legitimate and require careful consideration. This
chapter's presentation and discussion of reform objectives and results
should help to answer some of the questions. It is also important to
stress that at the time of writing these are still very early days for the
Putin regime. It is barely one year since Vladimir Putin was elected as
Russia's new president in a single round of voting on 26 March 2000.
By any realistic benchmark the positive change regarding economic
policy and governance in this short time has been notable compared
with most of the Yeltsin era, particularly the period after 1996. In the
words of two of the leading experts on, and participants in, Russia's
economic reforms and revolutionary changes: 'Previously, Russia had
been idealized in the West, and even its most obvious problems and
contradictions had been overlooked. By the end of the 1990s, in contrast, its negative features were being grotesquely exaggerated and
positive aspects were being completely ignored.'[4] With a critical mass
of structural and economic reforms now being pursued, chances are
that these perceptions will change in a more positive direction.

Indeed, Mau and Starodubrovskaya offer a good starting place in the
effort to put current developments in the right context. Vladimir Mau (a
leading participant in Russian reforms over the past decade and head of
the government's Working Centre for Economic Reform) and Irina
Starodubrovskaya (deputy director of the Foundation for Enterprise
Restructuring and Financial Institutions) have published a major treatise
on the process of revolution in Russia with a particular focus on the
period from 1985 to 2000. This book is likely to become a new land-
mark and focal point for discussion of Russian affairs and the process of
revolutionary changes and economic reforms in the country. The conclusions and insights arising from Mau and Starodubrovskaya's work
are of direct relevance for the current debate and for understanding the
evolution of Russian reforms.

One of the key elements of their book is an outline of how the revolutionary stage of Russia's developments in the 1990s has now transited to a post-revolutionary stage, during which Russia will gradually embark on the path of more evolutionary change. A number of aspects characterize this shift. First, a consolidation of the élite is under way, with the opposition becoming further marginalized. Second, the approach to economic policy has evolved, such that the choice of a market economy is beyond question and there are the beginnings of economic growth. Third, there have been no major social upheavals in response to the tightening in fiscal policy (this is also a reflection of the previous point). And fourth, there is evidence that society is tired of upheavals *per se*.

Moves to strengthen a weakened state, such as those undertaken by President Putin, should be seen as a natural ingredient of Russia's current evolution. Historical experience shows that a weak state is a (possibly the) key element of revolutionary upheavals, so that transition to a new post-revolutionary stage will almost always involve attempts at strengthening the over-weakened state and recapturing ability to implement policy decisions. In this context, the current process of bolstering the credibility and political capital of centralized institutions is not odd or unusual. Furthermore, historical analysis indicates that stable economic growth can be achieved only as the process moves into this post-revolutionary stage. However, it would be wrong to think that the further course of reforms in Russia will be smooth or simple. The point, rather, is that the challenges and constraints will be different.

One of the key challenges for Russia will be to establish itself as part of the current globalized international economy. Russian economic policy is focused on pursuing structural and institutional policies, targeting the emergence of sustainable economic growth. For this purpose, a core set of near-term reform challenges is being formulated and pursued. The road map ahead is very busy, and the government will be hard pressed to avoid either over-extending itself or falling into a trap of reform fatigue. President Putin's annual address to the Federal Assembly in spring 2001 could be seen as the start of a rejuvenated reform push. Prospects for fiscal policy and debt management reforms promise moves towards more transparency, efficiency and forward-looking macroeconomic policies.

Despite a slowdown from 2000, real GDP growth of 3–4 per cent is achievable for 2001 and the structure of growth is altering towards increased domestic demand and investment. The slowdown in economic growth cannot credibly be said to be *caused* by real appreciation of the rouble – exchange rate dynamics are a natural reflection of Russia's balance of payments and of the transformation process itself, and systematic attempts to resist the appreciation will worsen rather than improve the situation. The problem lies elsewhere, primarily in corporate restructuring and the absence of deep financial markets.

THE RUSSIAN ECONOMY: GROWTH AND INFLATION

As regards macroeconomic developments, two main issues are in focus – economic growth and inflation. On the former, some participants in the domestic Russian debate maintain that growth dynamics have not only weakened but turned into stagnation and decline. In addition, some have claimed that real appreciation of the rouble is the key danger for the Russian economy, implying that economic policy should favour a weaker rouble. In our analysis and treatment of the available data, we find the economic contraction claim unconvincing, the real appreciation story erroneous and the policy conclusion highly detrimental.

66some have claimed that real appreciation of the rouble is the key danger for the Russian economy, implying that economic policy should favour a weaker rouble.99

Our analysis, and other Russian economic research, indicates that if the level of GDP in 2001 stays flat from December 2000 levels, GDP growth would still be some 2–2.5 per cent.[5] A realistic range of growth estimates for Russia in 2001 would be between 2 and 2.5 per cent and 3.5 and 4 per cent. In its latest forecast, the Ministry of Economic Development and Trade expects full-year 2001 real GDP growth at 4 per cent.[6] In the context of a global growth slowdown, we do not regard such a moderation from near 8 per cent growth in 2000 as dramatically worrying, and we do not share the general perception of real appreciation as the main culprit for this slow-down. Instead, we would highlight the importance of economic policy and the reform process, especially with regard to confidence, credibility and sentiment. Below we outline these issues in more detail.

In January 2001, Goskomstat, the Russian statistical agency, reported year-on-year industrial production growth at 5.3 per cent (adjusted for the number of working days, the growth was 2 per cent), while the month-on-month decline was 5.4 per cent, which is not unusual for January, a month of many holidays. In February, industrial production was up a mere 0.8 per cent year-on-year, but adjusted for working days the increase was 4.9 per cent. Industrial production expanded by a modest 3.1 per cent in January and February together compared with the same period in 2000. According to preliminary data, in the first quarter of 2001 industrial production expanded by 3.3 per cent year-on-year, following March industrial production growth of 3.6 per cent year-on-year and 10.3 per cent month-on-month. While overall industrial production growth slowed down during the last part of 2000 and going into 2001, the structure of production dynamics is encouraging. Light industry was up 8.1 per cent year-on-year in the January–February period, machine-building grew by 5.2 per cent (one sub-category here is television sets, production of which was up 43.3 per cent), while energy increased only 2.1 per cent.

Other indicators also suggest continuation of economic growth, and point especially to overall GDP growth being stronger than industrial production growth.[7] In the January–February period, investments grew by 7.6 per cent, retail trade by 8 per cent and real incomes by 5.7 per cent. In the first quarter of 2001 year-on-year investment growth was 6.6 per cent, retail trade increased by 8.2 per cent and real incomes by 3.2 per cent. Goskomstat's index of so-called base sector output of goods and services, capturing 65 per cent of GDP, was up by 3.5 per cent in the January–February period, and 3.6 per cent in the first quarter year-on-year. In addition, given January and February export and import figures, it is likely that net exports will be up by close to 10 per cent year-on-year in the first quarter.[8] In line with this, the Ministry for Economic Development and Trade forecast that real GDP growth will reach 4.2 per cent for the first six months of 2001. However, the slow-down in investment growth needs to be watched carefully, as does the development of real incomes. Further slowdown in investments over the next quarter would be a worrying indicator, pertaining to expecta-tions and the level of confidence about the rate of improvement of the investment climate. Real income dynamics need to be followed closely as well, with higher-than-budgeted inflation eroding the outcome for the first quarter. However, it should be noted that retail trade remains almost as strong as in 2000.

We would also stress the interesting picture arising from enterprise sur-veys, which lend further support to the picture of growth picking up in February–March 2001, and continuing later in the year. It is clear that after a lull towards the end of 2000, enterprise expectations improved noticeably once again, which could be a leading indicator for a pick-up in growth later in the year.[9] As Figures 11.1 and 11.2 indicate, production expectations staged a clear recovery in January–March, as did expecta-tions of cash demand. Consumer surveys also testify to continued optimism. As Figure 11.2 indicates, consumer sentiment regarding current material well-being, expectations for the year ahead and the propensity to make large purchases all rose to new highs in January 2001.

Figure 11.1 *Enterprise surveys, April 1999–February 2001*

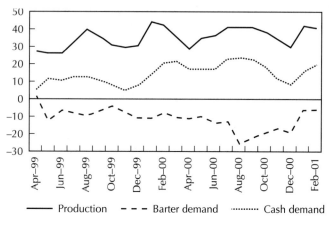

Source: IET.

The data points measure the difference between increase and decrease expectations for coming months.

Figure 11.2 *Consumer surveys, May 1996–January 2001 (VTSIOM survey indices)*

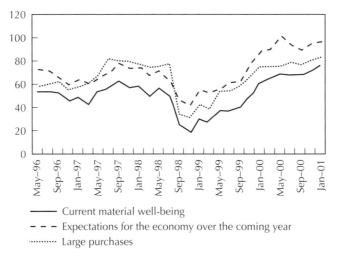

——— Current material well-being
– – – Expectations for the economy over the coming year
·········· Large purchases

Source: VTSIOM, Tsentr Razvitia

Real exchange rate appreciation and Russian economic growth

Thus, while there was undeniably a slowdown in the second half of 2000, mainly due to CIS import growth and PPI movements, signs of growth are still present in the Russian economy, although the pace has slackened. Quarter-on-quarter GDP expansion developed from +5 per cent in the first quarter of 2000 to +0.9 per cent and +1.4 per cent in the last two quarters of 2000 respectively. In the fourth quarter, the year-on-year GDP growth rate was 7.3 per cent, while annual real GDP growth came in at 7.6 per cent. Subsequent data revisions are likely to raise these figures further.

It is fashionable to attribute the slowdown in economic growth and even feared contraction to real appreciation of the rouble, with the transmission mechanism being a loss of competitiveness and evaporation of gains induced by the 1998 devaluation. The large current account surplus is often viewed as a part of this problem. We recognize that there is a relevant discussion regarding the extent and speed of real appreciation and its interaction with structural reforms and corporate restructuring. However, the insistence on making real appreciation and the current account surplus the main culprits for alleged evaporation of economic growth does not stand up to scrutiny and carries flawed policy conclusions. Rather, the focus should be on accepting real appreciation as a reflection of the transformation process, while pursuing financial system restructuring, acceleration of structural reforms and improvement of the investment climate.[10] Very little will be achieved through engineering a weaker rouble, and the result could well be to make the situation worse.

Before we go into some of these issues in more detail, two facts about rouble exchange rate dynamics need to be underlined. First, while the rouble certainly has appreciated in real terms, the gap between the market exchange rate and the PPP exchange rate remains large – larger than the corresponding difference in more advanced transition economies, for example. In addition, the real exchange rate is still well below its pre-1998 levels (see Figure 11.3). Even assuming a 10 per cent real appreciation for the year ending December 2001, the level of the (trade-weighted) real exchange rate would still be more than 20 per cent below the level of 1997. Second, the extent and speed of the real appreciation is not overly dramatic or unusual. In 2000, the trade-weighted real exchange appreciated by about 10.2 per cent, and in the first quarter of 2001 by 3.4 per cent (or 3.1 per cent if measured against the dollar). The stronger real appreciation in the first quarter of this year was due mainly to higher-than-expected inflation.

Figure 11.3 *The real (trade-weighted) and nominal exchange rate 1998–2000*

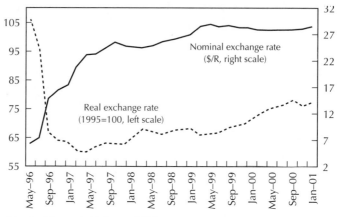

Source: Schroder Salomon Smith Barney, RECEP

In considering the role of real exchange rate appreciation in the process of Russian economic growth and reform, we would highlight a couple of aspects. First, given the current macroeconomic situation and the structural reforms being pursued, the rouble *has* to appreciate via either of two mechanisms – through a nominal appreciation trend or through the inflation differential in the context of a stable or moderately depreciating nominal exchange rate. The current account surplus remains very large, and despite continuing capital flight, the net supply of dollars to the rouble market is substantial. In addition, relative price adjustments (see more below) will put pressure on the CPI for some time as structural reforms are accelerated. Importantly, real exchange rate appreciation is an inherent and vital part of the process of catching up and restructuring in reforming transition economies, whether they are natural resource importers or natural resource exporters.[11]

In addition, real appreciation is a common phenomenon following a maxi-devaluation and financial crisis, as that experienced by Russia in late 1998. Second, the hypothesis that competitiveness is being eroded through excessive real appreciation of the rouble is equally unconvincing as an explanation of the growth slowdown. Russia's industrial competitiveness is not given primarily through the exchange rate and it is not lost primarily through the exchange rate. Looking at the *individual* costs of the factors of production, Russia is on paper a highly competitive economy. This has not changed significantly despite the gradual real appreciation of the rouble over the past couple of years.

66real exchange rate appreciation is an inherent and vital part of the process of catching up and restructuring in reforming transition economies99

Russia's competitiveness and productivity problems stem from the structural characteristics of the corporate sector, the real economy and the institutional set-up. Examples here would be *over-employment, all kinds of market distortions, lack of a transparent legal framework, insecure property rights*, and so on.[12] The key point is this: if there is a problem with competitiveness, it is not because of gradual real appreciation of the rouble but because of slow or problematic corporate restructuring. In this context, engineering a weaker rouble – assuming this could be done given the current macroeconomic fundamentals – would basically be a sign that the authorities were unconvinced about corporate restructuring and other institutional reforms which are under way. The benefits of such a policy are hard to see.[13] In addition, it should be pointed out that engineering a weaker rouble would, all else being equal, lead to a *higher*, not lower, external surplus.

Instead of ascribing Russian economic growth exclusively to factors such as the oil price and the exchange rate, or some combination thereof, one should not underestimate the importance of more generic factors such as accumulated enterprise adjustment. While indirect liquidity effects of improved external conditions have played an important role in 1999–2000, we would highlight the *combined* impact of external influences and the process of enterprise adaptation, corporate and consumer optimism, tighter budget constraints, and new international financial realities (reduced or zero IMF funds, firmer 'ownership' of the economic policy agenda). One of the leading and most insightful Russian economists and reformers, Professor Yegor Gaidar, has repeatedly made the point that while external factors account for a certain part of economic growth generated in 2000, the contribution from an inherent process of enterprise adaptation and restructuring, both accumulated over the years and proceeding at the moment, is substantial.[14]

If there is a problem with the connection between the exchange rate and economic growth, it lies not so much in real appreciation *per se* but in the combination of large external surpluses and thin financial markets together with an unrestructured financial system. In this regard, one relevant policy discussion is, as noted above, the extent and speed of the real appreciation. Because of thin financial markets and low financial intermediation between the financial sector and the real economy, there are few sterilization options for the Central Bank. In this environment the Central Bank has accumulated reserves to prevent over-rapid real appreciation, but this has led to additional money supply, which threatens to become an even more serious problem. So far, the bulk of the excess domestic liquidity has been soaked up through fiscal surpluses and CBR deposits. The lack of banking sector restructuring is a real problem, and there has been little to be optimistic about over the past couple of years.[15] The monetary authorities have not shown great interest in pursuing this issue. This, however, is not a problem of the real appreciation *per se*, and equally it cannot be blamed on the existence of a large current account surplus.

Another aspect that should be considered is the link between the exchange rate, the main exporters and domestic liquidity, and thus in-directly investment growth and monetization. Following the 1998 devaluation and the start of the oil price rise from the second quarter of 1999, Russian exporters received a double windfall gain – higher export prices and lower domestic costs, since the latter are denomi-nated in roubles. In the wake of this, the export sector started to meet domestic payments of various kinds (taxes, wages, pensions and sup-plier payments) at higher and higher degrees of cash component. This provided a positive jolt to domestic liquidity, which trickled down through the Russian economy. This process is one part of the story behind the near 18 per cent jump in investment growth in 2000. Since the current account will gradually shrink from here on, all else being equal, this channel will become less important. But again, this is not a case of real appreciation eroding competitiveness.

Based on January–March CPI indicators, it is likely that 2001 CPI will be 18–20 per cent rather than the 12–14 per cent previously expected by the government. The Russian government has acknowledged that budgeted inflation may have to be revised upwards.[16] This, however, will help rather than hurt the budget, as expenditures are fixed. As the country embarks on a series of major structural reforms, and as the CBR's sterilization options remain limited, relative price adjustments will exert pressure on Russian CPI for some time. A breakdown of the monthly CPI data for January–March 2001 emphasizes that price growth for services continues to be the dominating factor behind monthly inflation. Services price growth in the first quarter was 12.9 per cent (compared with 7.1 per cent overall CPI). Services inflation is driven by readjustment of municipal and electricity tariffs, both of which will see major relative price adjustments for some time as struc-tural reforms are accelerated.

The fiscal performance

The main fiscal event during February–March 2001 was the adoption of amendments to the 2001 budget, in order to mobilize additional revenues for debt service (to make full Paris Club payments and to substitute budgeted but non-realized International Financial Institution (IFI) funding). After some fairly tough discussions with the Duma, a compromise was found and necessary amendments were approved in three readings on February 22. In mid-March, the Federation Council approved the same amendments without problem in the required one reading. The amendments contain three main points: they allow additional domestic borrowing of R30 billion, allow use of some R33 billion from 2000 fiscal funds for debt service purposes, and establish that the first R41.2 billion of excess budget revenues will be channelled to debt service, with the subsequent R124 billion split 50/50 between debt service and non-interest expenditures.

According to Ministry of Finance estimates, the fiscal gap, which these amendments need to fill, is R182.95 billion. The ministry arrived at this figure by using conservative estimates of non-IMF IFI and bilateral funding. However, our analysis leads us to believe that the Russian government will have no problem covering this gap with the help of the budget amendments. We outline our base-case scenario in Table 11.1. The key parameter is the estimate of excess budget revenues. In politically sound fashion, the government initially predicted total excess budget revenues for 2001 at R108 billion. However, we expect the real excess to be closer to R200 billion. Table 11.1 is constructed assuming 2001 excess budget revenues at R200 billion.

Table 11.1 *Excess 2001 budget revenues – the distribution to debt service (assuming R200 billion excess revenues)*

	R billion
The first R41.2 billion of excess revenues to debt service	41.2
The subsequent R124 billion is divided 50/50 between debt service and non-interest spending	62
Excess revenues above R165.2 billion to debt service	34.8
Additional domestic borrowing	30
Funds transferred from year 2000, to be used for debt service	33
Total	**201**

Source: 2001 budget amendments, Ministry of Finance, Schroder Salomon Smith Barney

Early fiscal indicators for 2001 are encouraging, and indeed point to potential for substantial excess revenues. In January, normally not an active month in terms of economic activity and fiscal performance due to many holidays, federal revenues were nevertheless 4.1 per cent above the monthly target, while expenditures were 13.6 per cent below target. In February, federal budget revenues were 6 per cent over target, with expenditures 12.6 per cent below target. For March, preliminary data indicate federal fiscal revenue collection at 3.8 per cent above target, with expenditures 13.6 per cent below target.[17]

Note in particular that tax collection (by the Tax Ministry) was 6.8 per cent above target in March, and corresponded to some 11.7 per cent of GDP, an improvement of nearly two percentage points of GDP compared with January (see Table 11.2). Ministry of Finance preliminary first-quarter fiscal data point to total first-quarter tax collection at R195.3 billion and total first-quarter federal revenues at R318.8 billion, or 17.7 per cent of GDP. Given these figures, the government has raised second-quarter federal revenue targets by R51.8 billion compared with the initial 2001 budget (putting total predicted second-quarter revenues at R302.8 billion). The trend was thus already positive in the early months of the year. While these are still early days, one cannot completely discount the possibility of some positive influence already from the tax reforms adopted in 2000 and in effect from 1 January 2001 (e.g. the flat income tax rate of 13 per cent).[18] Indeed, the preliminary Ministry of Finance fiscal data show that personal income tax collection jumped about 70 per cent in the first quarter of 2001 compared with the first quarter of 2000.

Table 11.2 *Fiscal revenue performance – first quarter 2001*

	Actual performance, % of target
January federal budget revenue collection	104.1
January tax collection	106.5
February federal budget revenue collection	106.0
February tax collection	105.1
March federal budget revenue collection	103.8
March tax collection	106.8

Source: Ministry of Finance, Schroder Salomon Smith Barney.
Federal budget revenue collection includes tax and non-tax revenues. Tax collection refers to the bulk of taxes, collected under the control of the Tax Ministry.

The exchange rate outlook and financial system restructuring

After a stable performance in January, the rouble weakened in February–April 2001. However, we do not see this as a major shift in the exchange rate outlook. The fundamental fact about the Russian foreign exchange market is that the Central Bank controls it effectively and is able to bring the currency pretty much to the level it wants, while continuing to accumulate reserves. As per 30 March, CBR reserves stood at $29.7 billion, and we expect reserves to end the year at about $35 billion. As noted above, the trade-weighted rouble real exchange rate appreciated by 3.4 per cent in the first quarter of 2001. Given April–May inflation outcomes, the CBR may decide to guide the rouble lower yet again. On the revised inflation outlook, the rouble will nevertheless end the year at around R31–32 to the dollar, corresponding to an 8–10 per cent real appreciation. Despite intra-month movements, the Central Bank remains sceptical in principle about a 'weak rouble' policy and would prefer a stronger rouble.

This has been confirmed by CBR governor Viktor Geraschenko, who has emphasized that the Central Bank sees more risks than benefits from a 'weak rouble' policy, and that the task of the CBR on the forex market would continue to be avoidance of any sharp movements. At the same time, the CBR will not explicitly strive for a stronger rouble, and will be ready to continue dollar buying to prevent excessively sharp appreciation. In general, exchange rate policy is squeezed between the need to prevent over-rapid real appreciation and concerns over monetary consequences of reserve accumulation in the environment of thin financial markets. The lobbies of exporters and domestic producers, who prefer a softer rouble, are not unimportant, but the government, while also interested in keeping the extent of real appreciation manageable, benefits from a gradual real appreciation as it alleviates the external debt burden and, as we have discussed above, a policy of explicitly engineering a weaker rouble would carry substantial risks.

66the Central Bank remains sceptical in principle about a 'weak rouble' policy and would prefer a stronger rouble.99

Contrary to what is perhaps the general perception, our conversations with Russian officials suggest that Russia is moving towards acceptance of the combination of rouble real appreciation and reform acceleration. In the short term this means a tough fight against selected vested interests calling for a 'weak rouble policy', but it is the best course for the government and ultimately also for the real economy. The external debt burden will moderate, a certain push for enterprise restructuring will be present, reform acceleration will help rating upgrades, and the pay-off to structural reforms will come over the medium term. Indeed, in the macroeconomic assumptions underlying the government's draft 2002–4 macroeconomic action plan, it is assumed that the rouble will continue to follow a path of gradual real appreciation.

A focus over coming weeks and months will be reform and restructuring of the financial system, which has been the most disappointing aspect of economic reform up to now. Encouragingly, signs are that the government is intent on moving this process forward, hopefully pushing the more reluctant Central Bank to move ahead as well.

Specifically, the government, the Duma and the Kremlin now appear to more or less agree on the road map for a set of crucial amendments to three separate banking laws making up what is known as the 'IMF package'. This package is composed of amendments to the law on bank bankruptcy, the law on banking activity and the law on the Central Bank. The full adoption of these amendments has for some time constituted a key IMF prior action. On 23 March 2001, the Duma banking committee decided to recommend parliament to approve the above amendments in a second reading, and the amendments were passed by the Duma in a second reading on 18 April. There are other signs of a new focus on financial system reforms. In late February, the Duma approved a second reading of legislation which exempts bills issued by the Central Bank from taxation. This is part of a process of enabling resumption of Central Bank bill issuance, as a liquidity-regulating instrument. We expect this process to be concluded by the end of 2001. Separately, the relevant agencies and ministries are expected to submit to the government a draft law on deposit insurance. This will be preceded by ongoing discussions and work on banking sector restructuring under the auspices of the Ministry for Economic Development and Trade.

The government and the Kremlin are also moving towards currency regime liberalization, specifically (but not exclusively) with regard to the rule on obligatory sale of hard-currency revenue. Representatives of both the government and the Kremlin have indicated that they will soon move to lower obligatory sales from the current 75 per cent of revenues to around 50–40 per cent, and then later to 20–40 per cent, with the possibility of complete abolition at a later stage. However, since the Central Bank leadership is far more cautious in this issue, we expect any liberalization of the currency regime to be gradual and careful.

ECONOMIC POLICY: THE CURRENT AGENDA

Russia's economic policy debate revolves around three issues: priority economic policy measures for the remainder of 2001, the short-term economic action programme for 2002–4 and the 2002 budget, and codification of a long-term economic strategy (to 2010) via a presidential decree.

On 1 March 2001, the Russian government reviewed the main macro-economic outcomes of 2000 and focused on the challenges for 2002–4, including measures for the remainder of 2001. This was an opportunity to emphasize the pursuit of structural reforms, a struggle the government has sought to revive over the past few months. Our basic assessment is this: following the successful launch in summer 2000 of the economic strategy drafted under the auspices of the Minister for Economic Development and Trade, German Gref, and the positive achievements of the first phase of tax and centre-regional fiscal reforms, there was a near standstill in economic policy during late 2000 and early 2001.[19] This was partly because the government was risking 'over-extending' itself – the list of structural reform priorities had grown very long and a further round of prioritizing and sequencing the necessary political coalition building seemed to be needed.[20]

The importance of prioritizing is a key point. On one hand there is a general perception of Russian reforms as glacier-like in their speed, piecemeal and/or unconvincing. On the other hand there have been suggestions that the Putin regime should *not* use its accumulated political capital to pursue reforms, but rather try not to 'rock the boat'. Whereas the former perception is perhaps a symptom of unrealistic expectations, the suggestion that reform efforts at present are undesirable is particularly misleading. It is easy to pursue reforms when times are bad. It is when times are good that reform momentum becomes difficult to maintain. And it is precisely in good times that the Russian establishment needs to prove its ability to formulate priorities and move forward on these priorities. In our analysis, the problem has not been the speed of reforms (expectations here have been too unrealistic) but the scale of declared ambitions and the length of the reform wish-list combined with the limited administrative ability of the bloated Russian ministerial bureaucracy.

A wide reform focus is laudable for its ambition, but it may complicate achievement of a more narrow set of reforms of higher importance. During February, March and early April 2001, the government and the Kremlin gradually showed a new willingness to revive the pursuit of crucial economic reforms. In particular, new focus was injected by President Putin's strongly pro-reform annual address to the Federal Assembly on 3 April, in which he urged acceleration of structural economic reforms and lent his support to many of the ideas pursued by key reformers in the government. Another example would be the overwhelming Duma approval on 4 April of new profit tax legislation in a first reading. It is also encouraging that President Putin created a special working group on 9 April to present measures by July for a phased liberalization of the Gazprom share market, as well as calling for greater transparency and efficiency in Gazprom. A further positive indication is approval in the first reading of the new version of the Arbitration-Process Code by a large Duma majority. This act is part of a substantial package of legal and judicial reforms, whose impact will be to improve the investment climate by making the legal system more transparent and efficient.

The need for careful coalition building in each of the key reform issues should not be underestimated. President Putin still enjoys strong popularity, but institutional and economic reforms require the crafting of workable political-administrative coalitions and consensus.[21] In this context, we welcome signs that the Russian government is moving towards outlining a core set of reforms which will be pushed to conclusion over the remainder of 2001. This does not mean other reform priorities are discarded, but it does mean that the chances of success are enhanced for the near-term key priorities, thanks to concentrated and more efficient use of the authorities' political capital. It might also serve to introduce a more realistic benchmark against which Russian progress can be judged. We would like to call this identifying and achieving *the critical mass of structural reform progress.* By implication, we would identify four main areas which the Russian authorities are crystallizing as main near-term challenges.

1 *Business deregulatory reforms and the second phase of tax reform.*

While complex and intricate, these are reforms of huge importance.[22] They pertain to the nuts and bolts of doing business in Russia, whether for domestic or foreign investors. These reforms constitute the second major reform step after last summer's progress with the Tax Code. They are drafted and directed under the auspices of German Gref's Ministry for Economic Development and Trade (like most of the recent reforms). The cost to the Russian economy of excessive licensing, bureaucratic barriers to business and similar practices is huge. For example, there are 500 activities which require licensing on the federal level and another 600–700 which require licensing on a regional level (the regional licences are actually illegal since they have no support in federal legislation). The main idea behind the crucial initiative is to cut the number of federally required licences from around 500 to about 100.

The Ministry for Economic Development and Trade estimates that these practices cost the Russian economy R200 billion per year, or around $5 billion (more than the annual Paris Club debt service). Specifically, the first package of business reforms and debureaucratization measures consists of three main law drafts:

■ on the protection of legal persons and individual entrepreneurs in the context of government controls;

■ on government registration of legal persons;

■ amendments to the law on licensing.

On 2 March 2001, an extraordinary cabinet meeting approved two of the above three drafts, and on 15 March the government approved the licensing amendments. The initiative has been passed by the Duma. Later, going into 2002, a second package of business reforms will be prepared.

The main element of the second phase of tax reforms is the new profit tax draft. After a large amount of work and compromise consultations, the draft was submitted to the Duma on 19 March. In an encouraging sign, the new profit tax was swiftly approved by an overwhelming Duma majority before its summer break. The other main part of this second phase of tax reforms is a new tax on natural resource extraction, as well as possible new regulations affecting transfer pricing practices. As with profit tax, the new tax on natural resource extraction was also passed before the Duma's summer recess.

2 *The new Land Code and private ownership of land.*

At a meeting of the State Council (Gossovet) on 21 February 2001, President Putin outlined the road map in this issue and re-emphasized the importance of settling the question of private ownership of land. On 26 April, the Kasyanov government submitted the new Land Code to the Duma. The Land Code was approved in the second reading before the summer recess. The summer will be spent preparing for the third readings during the autumn and winter session. Furthermore, the government was mandated to draft a separate law by June on the treatment of agricultural land. Such a law might be adopted by the Duma in 2002.

The immediate economic impact of a new Land Code is less important than its political and symbolic content. However, it would play a role fairly soon as part of debt-for-equity-and-investment proposals to restructure Russia's Soviet-era debt.

3 *Reforms of the legal and judicial system.*

Another process which over time should have a major impact on the investment climate is a wide-ranging reform of the legal and court system, prepared under the auspices of Dmitry Kozak, one of the deputy heads of the presidential administration. The idea is to make the legal system more professional and less prone to corruption. The Duma's overwhelming approval of a new version of the Arbitration-Process Code (on 12 April) was a major step towards this goal. The change strengthens the independence of arbitration courts and makes the sole venue for hearing economic cases and cases involving foreign companies. This would go a long way towards dealing with some of the problems which have arisen over the years when such cases are heard in other, non-arbitration, courts.

Another part of this reform package is a new version of the Civil-Process Code, a first reading of which is expected late April or May, as well as a new law on the status of courts. In December, the most controversial part of the judicial reform programme, the new Criminal-Process Code, might be ready for a reading.

4 *UES restructuring and reform.*

The special working group set up to draft a UES restructuring programme missed its 15 April 2001 deadline, but the group and the relevant authorities involved will probably present a compromise restructuring programme by the last weeks of April. The Kremlin and President Putin will then determine the next steps to be taken, and we could hopefully see the initiation of the restructuring process shortly. A political decision by the Kremlin is expected by 16 May.

The first group of reforms, aimed at removing obstacles to business, is crucial. The government will need its political capital and determination to guide these reforms through parliament, and success will be an important indicator of its political stamina in pursuing prioritized economic reforms, as we have noted. German Gref, who will be the minister ultimately in charge of steering the drafts through Duma readings, will be strengthened by a couple of factors. First, Putin's annual address to the Federal Assembly contained a notable re-affirmation of his support for these kinds of measures. Second, some Duma forces are rallying to support Gref's measures, and a special cross-party Duma structure of 55 deputies has been formed, called 'Delovaya Rossiya' or 'Business Russia'. The specific purpose of this new group is to support

Gref in pushing his business reforms. Also, the failure of a vote of no confidence in the government gave a reminder of the change in the political balance, towards the centre and centre-right. The decision to further consolidate the Kremlin-supportive political centre, through a co-ordinating council between four factions – Unity, Fatherland, Russian Regions and People's Deputy – is part of this process.

In addition to this core set of reforms, the government is in various stages of preparing a long list of other measures, such as a new Customs Code (to be submitted shortly to the Duma, most likely during the autumn parliamentary session), a new Labour Code (a government-Duma working group is drafting a version, and Duma officials predict that it might be presented in a full Duma session by the summer recess), a reworked system of fiscal federalism and centre-regional budget relations (to be submitted shortly to the government by the Ministry of Finance and discussed by the full cabinet on 23 May) and pension reforms. Also, reform of the state railways monopoly (the Railways Ministry) is approaching. On 19 March, a reform concept prepared partly by McKinsey was more or less approved by the Railways Ministry and Gref's Ministry for Economic Development and Trade, and was discussed by the government in April.

> **the failure of a vote of no confidence in the government gave a reminder of the change in the political balance, towards the centre and centre-right.**

Another vital factor for the investment climate is the introduction of a Code of Corporate Governance, which is being driven by the Federal Securities Commission under the leadership of its chairman, Igor Kostikov. The expectation is that this code will be fully drafted in 2001. Importantly, this process has the government's support, as confirmed by Prime Minister Mikhail Kasyanov. An indication of this was the government's submission to the Duma on 24 April of a set of special legal amendments to the Criminal Code with regard to the securities markets. These amendments are sponsored by the Federal Securities Commission, and would significantly tighten the sanctions against various shareholder rights violations.

The Russian government's long-term economic programme (up until 2010), augmented and amended from last year's version, was reviewed in a special briefing with Prime Minister Kasyanov on 7 March 2001 and generally approved on 22 March. Signs are that President Putin has agreed to codify the programme in the form of a presidential decree following another round of intra-governmental discussions. As before, the programme places its key emphasis on improving the investment climate. There are four main observations to make regarding the amended and reworked economic strategy.

- The focus on targeting the emergence of sustainable economic growth via pursuit of major and comprehensive institutional and structural economic reforms is maintained and re-emphasised.

- Budget, exchange rate and debt issues take centre-stage in terms of macroeconomic policy. Notably, there is a movement towards emphasizing the need to change, modernize and add transparency to the budget process as a way of dealing with the external debt problem.

- An explicit policy of a weak rouble as surrogate economic policy is not embraced, rather it is held up as a worst-case outcome. A gradual rouble real appreciation will be assumed.

- There is stronger accent on the need to actively engage the Central Bank in financial system reforms, such as reform of the banking system, the currency regulatory regime and monetary policy.

The Kasyanov government has also outlined some specific budget, debt policy and other measures to be taken during the remainder of 2001. The measures below are in addition to the 2002 budget preparation process and the task of preparing a forward-looking, fiscal plan for the period up to and including 2004 (see more on this overleaf).

- The Ministry for Economic Development and Trade is mandated to co-ordinate a methodology for a full evaluation of the economic situation and investment potential of Russia's regions.

- The ministry is also ordered to complete work in the second quarter on normative legal acts regarding business activity.

- The ministry is mandated to draft and submit a new federal law on regulating external trade activities to the government by the fourth quarter.

- The Ministry of Finance is ordered to present a report to the government in the fourth quarter on results of budget expenditure reforms and progress in tax reforms.

- The Ministry of Finance is mandated to take measures to regulate Soviet-era external debt, and to present a report to the government on the results by the fourth quarter.

- Relevant ministries are mandated to draft and present proposals by 1 September 2001 on enhancing the efficiency of companies in which the state holds a stake of more than 50 per cent.

- Relevant ministries are ordered to draft and present proposals by 1 July for restructuring of bankrupt enterprises in which the state has ownership stakes.

ECONOMIC POLICY AND INVESTMENTS: SELECTED ISSUES

Above we have identified and discussed some of the key economic policy initiatives being pursued. If pursued resolutely, these initiatives are likely to have a major impact on investment activity over time, both on private domestic investments and foreign investments to the Russian economy. Below we discuss some selected issues in the economic policy/investment nexus facing Russia, such as credit ratings, the need to reform the debt management system, the state of foreign direct investments, and the main dynamics of private domestic investments.

Credit ratings

Table 11.3 summarizes Russia's ratings from the three main agencies. Following the collapse of ratings in the aftermath of 1998, Russia gained a ratings rehabilitation momentum in 2000, which continued in the first quarter of 2001. Given the current macroeconomic situation and the policy path, it is likely that this momentum will continue over the next couple of years. Moody's is likely to upgrade Russian eurobonds to B2 at least this year, once the level of comfort with the Paris Club situation solidifies. The latest move by S&P's in early March was a rather surprising decision to put eurobonds and all MinFins (4–8) except non-exchanged MinFin 3 at the same rating level of B–.

SSSB's 'shadow rating' or value opinion places Russia as a mid-B credit. In Figure 11.4, the SSSB sovereign credit and ratings analysts have modelled the relationship between ratings and spreads for a number of emerging market countries.[23] The model has an R-square of 70 per cent. As can be seen, Russia comes out as an underrated country given where we see the rating potential, with the market pricing Russia closer to a mid-B than B–.

Table 11.3 *Russia's credit ratings, April 2001*

	Moody's	S&P	Fitch
Foreign currency ratings			
Long-term ceiling for bonds (Moody's)/issuer credit ratings (S&P & Fitch)	B2	B–	B
Short-term ceiling for bonds (Moody's)/issuer credit ratings (S&P & Fitch)	NP	B–	B
Long-term ceiling for bank deposits (Moody's only)	B3	–	–
Short-term ceiling for bank deposits (Moody's only)	NP	–	–
Eurobonds	B3(ru)	B–	B
MinFin 6,7	B3	B–	CCC+
MinFin 4,5	Caa3	B–	CCC
MinFin 8 (MinFin 8 is not rated by Moody's)	N/R	B–	CCC
MinFin 3 (non-exchanged)	Ca	W/D	–
Local currency ratings			
Long-term bond ratings (OFZs)	B3	B–	B–
Short-term bond ratings (GKOs)	NP	C	B

Source: Moody's Investors Service, S&P, Fitch

Note: (ru) indicates on review for possible upgrade.

Figure 11.4 *Spread and rating – emerging market bonds*

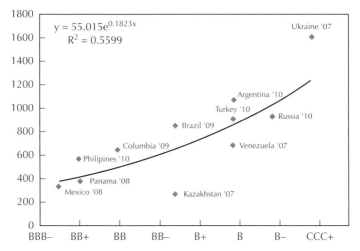

Source: SSSB Sovereign Credit Research, S&P, Moody's

Foreign direct investments

Tables 11.4 and 11.5 show the track record of foreign direct investments. These have been and remain very low for a country the size of Russia. The cumulative FDI stock in 2000 was no more than $141 per capita, well below, for example, the leading transition economies in central Europe but also behind countries in south-eastern Europe. As with the difference between PPP and market exchange rate GDP, this could be interpreted as major unrealized potential should Russia earn the confidence of FDI investors over the next couple of years. If Russia's growth recovery continues throughout Putin's first term (new elections are due in 2004), one would expect a gradual pick-up in FDI from 2002 (2001 may still be fairly modest due to the need for a longer track record to be established). However, there are already signs of new FDI trends, albeit somewhat anecdotal at this stage. In particular there are indications of large foreign firms eyeing both the Russian domestic market and the potential for domestic sourcing more resolutely than in the past. Examples here would be the expansion plans of Swedish furniture group IKEA, the decision of the French retailer Auchan to enter the Russian market, as well as similar plans by other international retailers, and the go-ahead for further joint projects in the Russian car industry.

Table 11.4 *Foreign direct investments to Russia 1993–2000*

	FDI (cumulative stock, $ billion)
1993	1.211
1994	1.85
1995	3.866
1996	6.345
1997	12.984
1998	15.745
1999	18.635
2000	21.135

Source: WIIW Database, Goskomstat, CBR

Table 11.5 *Per capita foreign direct investments, Eastern Europe and the CIS (sample), 2000 stock*

	FDI cumulative stock 2000, $ per capita
Russia	141
Hungary	1900
Poland	828
Czech	1752
Bulgaria	416
Ukraine	77
Macedonia	248

Source: WIIW Database, Goskomstat, CBR

Of course, individually these signs are not new. For example, there has already been a selected foreign presence in the retail market. However, the emergence of a broader critical mass seems to be occurring. Similar trends, although at a much earlier stage, can be seen in the foreign element of the Russian banking sector, with growth expected soon in the small number of foreign banks attempting to initiate retail consumer banking.

It is interesting to note that these FDI trends are being accompanied by vital signs of a domestic-led consolidation in both export and non-export sectors. For example, having embarked last year on a major consolidation of the Russian aluminium industry, large Russian metals interests have this year begun acquisitions in the car industry, notably in Nizhny Novgorod. Another example could be the Russian domestic confectionery industry, which is also undergoing a consolidation process.

Debt management reforms and debt ratios

Alongside an improving fiscal situation and a promising evolving debate on more forward-looking fiscal policy (see below), debt management has increasingly been in focus over the past year. Debt management reforms are now a more active ingredient in an overall interest from the Russian side in retaining and developing a constructive dialogue with private international capital markets. Given the ratings upgrade process described above, Russian authorities are wary of upsetting the rehabilitation momentum amid growing probability of new market access in 2002–3. The process of reforming Russian debt management into a more efficient and transparent operation is proceeding along four main paths.

- Continued work on regularizing hitherto unsettled Soviet-era debt, both external and domestic debt. This includes implementation of a core Foreign Trade Organization bond exchange (possibly to be implemented in the autumn 2001), further progress towards regularization of the International Merchant Bank / International Bank for Economic Cooperation issue (potentially in connection with the FTO bond exchange), and further moves to deal with various domestic debt categories from the late-Soviet period, which are still unresolved.

- A full inventory review of financial assets and liabilities of the Russian Federation, being conducted by the Ministry of Finance. This is expected by end-May/early-June. This is important, since a clearer picture regarding existing assets and liabilities will help in formulating the most appropriate fiscal and debt management policies.

- Giving fiscal and debt policy an important role in the 2002–4 macroeconomic action plan. As emphasized by President Putin, this involves a shift towards focus on measures to enable Russia to service its debt in full even during the debt service peak, while still pursuing consultations with official bilateral creditors on a possible debt rescheduling, should that be necessary in light of economic conditions.

■ Reforming the debt management system into a more efficient and transparent operation, preferably via unification of external and domestic debt management into one platform, as well as creating a national debt agency as the main analytical, strategic and tactical debt centre. The idea is clear – to improve the structure of debt liabilities and decrease the cost of debt service.

The Ministry of Finance external debt team has pursued these aims in a professional manner for some time and received a substantial political boost when President Putin outlined his support for debt management reforms.[24] More specifically, the plan to reform Russia's debt management system includes a move to establish Vneshekonombank as a commercial bank and to separate out VEB's function as the government's external debt agent to a separate national debt agency – the Debt Agency of the Russian Federation (DARF). These measures are due to be formally adopted by the end of 2001, and the whole process of setting up the new system could take another 12–24 months. Creation of a special monitoring system of non-government liabilities, such as regional debt, will be part of this process. The next step is to finalize drafting of the necessary government resolutions and presidential decrees which, as noted, has been given extra impetus following Putin's support. VEB has submitted drafts of the resolutions and decrees, but some further consultations and negotiations with the Ministry of Finance might be needed in order to iron out details of issues such as the exact jurisdiction of the debt agency, as well as the likelihood of a unified domestic and external debt platform. Regarding the latter, it is notable that President Putin has specifically stressed that 'a unified system of government debt management' needs to be established.

> **66 the plan to reform Russia's debt management system includes a move to establish Vneshekonombank as a commercial bank 99**

Improving debt ratios are also an indication of the process of rating rehabilitation. A look at some key debt ratios will underline the potential for significant improvements as a result of more transparent and efficient Russian debt management. Table 11.6 presents five important ratios, pertaining to both the evolution of the debt stock and to Russia's liquidity situation. Notably, it shows that Russia does not really have, and did not have, a

Table 11.6 *Russia's debt ratios 1996–2002 (external debt service)*

	Reserves (months of imports)	Debt/GDP	Debt/exports of goods & services	Debt service ratio	Debt service/ Fed.revenues
1996	3.0	33.4	138.4	14.5	30
1997	3.0	34.2	149.0	16.0	30
1998	2.5	57.6	187.0	28.0	89
1999	3.8	94.2	191.0	11.9	41
2000	7.5	61.0	137.0	9.8	28
2001	8.1	55.0	140.0	10.0	25
2002	9.7	51.0	147.0	10.5	23

Source: CBR, Ministry of Finance, SSSB

Average rouble–dollar rate per period. SSSB estimates and forecasts for 2001–2.

major external debt problem *per se*. While debt/GDP ballooned in 1999, this was mainly an exchange-rate effect. Rather, Russia's problems in the 1990s were related to liquidity and poor economic policy – reserves were mostly stagnant despite non-trivial external surpluses, a sign of substantial capital outflows. Whereas the economy's overall debt ratios were not a significant cause for anxiety before 1998, the federal authorities had major problems capturing a share of the resources being generated in the economy (for example via reserves or tax collection).

Over the past couple of years, however, the direction has been clear – tax discipline has improved significantly and capital flight (in a relative sense) has decreased, allowing for reserve accumulation (although reserves in months of imports are flattered by an import collapse in 1999) and improving ratios. The key ratio beyond the short term is annual debt service to federal budget revenues (the last column). During the 1990s, apart from the 1998–9 crisis, roughly between a quarter and a third of federal revenues went to debt service. This is clearly unsustainable for a long period of time, especially for a transition economy seeking to implement a range of structural reforms. The main continuous improvement in this ratio, however, is likely to come from a gradual increase in collection through better incentives such as those introduced by the current tax reforms, as well as significant restructuring and rationalization of the expenditure side.[25] We forecast that debt service could already be down to about 23 per cent of federal revenues by 2002.

However, while we expect Russia to continue on a path of debt normalization, the Paris Club will remain a source of uncertainty. The Russian side cannot rule out the possibility that, if it indeed gets a Paris Club deal by 2002–3, the Paris Club will ask for treatment comparable to the MinFin 4–5 (supposing that the relevant consolidation windows imply). Nevertheless, our judgement is that the official sector would not reject considering broader options in such a situation, e.g. if by then new money is being provided by private creditors via new market access, or using an analysis of past restructurings. It also remains our impression that should the Russian side at some point seriously consider a bond restructuring of the MinFin 4–5, such a restructuring would be done in the most market-constructive way possible.

Economic policy, private investments and growth

Ultimately, the main idea behind the government's efforts at improving the investment climate is to provide the necessary conditions for productivity growth and to attract more private investments – primarily domestic but with no discrimination against foreign investment – as well as to reduce capital flight. Considering the current state of affairs, resolution of the problems facing the country will require rapid economic growth based on greater production efficiency, the creation of a qualitatively new economic structure, and modernization of the economy. This must occur against the backdrop of a further progressive opening-up of the country, and its finding a new place in the global economy. Russian laws and the experience of enforcing these laws are such that at present the Russian economy is mostly open at the exit points [26] but closed at the entry points, due to powerful limiting factors such as arbitrary bureaucratic control and corruption. The opening-up of the economy should proceed not only through enhancement of the legislative base with a view to creating a state that is strong in legal respects and capable of guaranteeing stability in the country but also through the elimination of unnecessary bureaucratic hurdles, and through efforts to combat corruption and criminal activity. This has been noted above. In this section, we look at some selected issues in connection with fixed capital formation over the past couple of years, near-term challenges of financing, and sectoral specifics of the investment process.

The near 18 per cent growth in domestic investments last year was financed primarily out of retained earnings and inter-company loans. Nearly half of investments were financed from corporate profits, with bank financing accounting for a small share, and the share of bank credits in total investments even decreasing relative to 1999. As shown in Table 11.7, inter-company financing went up in 2000. The share of various budget levels (federal, local, municipal) and extra-budgetary funds is still quite substantial, at about a quarter of total investment. The structure of investment financing is yet another reason why improvement of the investment climate is vital. If the financial conditions of the real sector were to deteriorate, [27] there would immediately be a negative impact on investments. The slowdown in growth in late 2000 and early 2001, and the moderation of investment growth, is one aspect of this.

The investment financing structure in 2000 highlights the challenge of financial system restructuring. Bank restructuring will have to be among government priorities in the next few years, along with the improvement of the investment climate. However, it should be stressed that the lack of financial intermediation is not solely a problem of an under-developed and distorted banking system. It is largely a problem of confidence in government policies.

The sectoral composition of fixed investments also raises several questions. As indicated by statistics, nearly half of total investments (47.9 per

Table 11.7 *Sources of fixed investment in January–September 2000 and January–September 1999 (percent)*

	2000	1999
Total fixed investments	100.0	100.0
of which:		
From own sources	49.3	53.5
Outside capital	50.7	46.5
of which:		
Bank credits	3.3	5.7
From other companies	8.1	5.5
From budgets	21.7	17.6
From extra-budget funds	4.4	9.5
Other	13.2	8.2

Source: Goskomstat

cent in January–September 2000, to be more precise) was absorbed by the energy sector and transportation. That is quite natural given the high profits of those two sectors. The energy sector benefited from high world market prices for its exports, and transportation benefited from advantages created from its monopoly position. In 1999, the share of the energy sector and transportation in total investment was also high, but much lower than in 2000, at about 40 per cent of total fixed investments. It should be noted that the transportation and energy sectors produce less than 20 per cent of GDP (at domestic prices).[28] Thus, at present only half of total investment is allocated in the rest of economy, which includes manufacturing, services, agriculture and other sectors. This is a further reason why the creation of an overall attractive investment climate and the removal of constraints for private capital formation and productivity growth should play a crucial role in the government's economic strategy.

As we have noted earlier, the focus on investment climate improvement, reforms to enable productivity growth, and structural and institutional reforms is particularly important for a resource-rich economy such as Russia. Several studies [29] have shown how resource-poor countries have performed better than resource-rich countries. In resource-poor countries, new sectors of the economy were developed (telecommunications, information technology, etc.), while resource-rich countries were mostly extracting resources and transporting them. In resource-rich countries, export earnings were mostly kept offshore and were not repatriated. For obvious reasons political regimes in most such countries were quite supportive of domestic exporters. Thus, resource-rich economies suffered from permanent capital outflows.

> **Russia is a clear case of the developmental and growth problems of resource-rich countries.**

Russia is a clear case of the developmental and growth problems of resource-rich countries. Energy exporters have continued to take money offshore since the early 1990s, with capital flight from Russia reaching nearly 10 per cent of GDP in 1999 and remaining high in 2000. In dollar terms capital flight will be even higher in 2000 than in 1999, while it will probably remain at the same level as a percentage of GDP due to real growth and appreciation of the rouble.

It is important to look at recent Soviet and Russian history in this context. During the second half of the 20th century, Soviet growth rates slowed down as new deposits of oil and gas were developed, although the hydrocarbon wealth gave the Brezhnev regime a new lease of life for a while. There were increasing investments in the energy sector and transportation (mostly pipeline transportation). The Soviet planning authorities tended to allocate more and more investments to mining, while other sectors, which could potentially have produced more value added, suffered from under-financing. Thus, growth of investments in the energy sector in present-day Russia can be considered as a positive sign only if it occurs in the context of a major push for improvement of the general investment climate and the development of other sectors through productivity growth and the attraction of private capital formation.

Encouraging a shift over time towards an economic structure less dominated by the energy sector is implicit in the government's economic strategy. Indeed, the medium to long-term economic growth rates targeted in the strategy will require a quite different structure of the economy, less dependent on exports of energy and semi-finished products, or sectors with low value-added. The task of improving the investment climate and introducing the right incentives for private business investment is thus also crucial for economic restructuring and the renovation of capital stock from this perspective.

Despite the positive macroeconomic outcomes in 1999–2000 and the encouraging re-focus of economic policy, one cannot fail to notice that capital outflows continued and continue at a substantial rate. Capital flight has decreased as a share of the current account surplus but continues at significant levels in absolute terms. The turnaround in confidence and expectations takes time to achieve, and business is keeping a close eye on the Russian government and the Putin regime for signs of the depth of their commitment to structural reforms and improvement of the investment climate. Given the lack of confidence in government policies, capital flight from Russia reflects perfectly rational investor behaviour, both in the past and the present.

Capital flight can also be explained by macroeconomic factors. Real interest rates are one such factor. In 2000, real interest rates became negative. Deposit rates offered by commercial banks, for instance, vary around 5 per cent. Rates on deposits in the Central Bank are also low (9 per cent). Insignificant amounts of government securities were issued, and they traded at quite low yields. At the same time inflation reached 20.2 per cent for the year. There was an acceleration of inflation in mid-year due to rapidly growing reserves as the monetary authorities were unable to carry out proper sterilization policies. Thus in the autumn average inflation increased to around 2 per cent per month. In this situation, negative interest rates can be considered as a natural sterilization mechanism, induced by the markets. Investors have been hard-pushed to place their money in Russia since there are no attractive financial instruments.[30] Depositing money in the Russian banking systems means losing money.[31] Fixed investment thus remains as the only legal possibility to preserve money domestically. Bringing money offshore can be considered as another rational option, though illegal. But legal constraints have proved unable to do the job of flawed macroeconomic policies by keeping money in Russia.

The electricity sector deserves special attention in the context of economic policy and growth. The key point is that low electricity tariffs represent substantial indirect subsidies to the rest of the economy. Tariffs, which are subject to administrative regulation, increased by only 14 per cent in 1999, while PPI for the whole of industry grew 67 per cent during the same period. Payments for electricity accounted for 11.6 per cent of total material expenditures in Russian industry in 1999. In January–September 2000 electricity tariffs grew faster than PPI (37 per cent and 25.3 per cent respectively), but this was not enough to compensate for the gap that appeared in 1999. The power monopoly, UES, significantly improved its financial situation in 2000, largely due to stronger payment discipline (including supply cuts to debtors), but not due to relative price increases. Electricity consumers are still benefiting from low tariffs,[32] and electricity consumption in Russia remains excessive by international standards. At the same time, the age structure of fixed capital in the electricity sector is deteriorating sharply since this industry was substantially under-invested in the 1990s. Russian economic output became nearly 30 per cent more electricity intensive during the reform period. Some relative improvements are expected in 2000.

Thus the government intends to launch restructuring of UES as early as possible (a political decision is expected by 16 May, as noted above). Generally speaking UES restructuring envisages liberalization of electricity prices and establishment of competition between power stations. It is expected that the price shock will not be significant. At present electricity producers still have substantial under-utilized capacities and the potential supply of electricity is still much higher than demand. The situation will become much more grave if restructuring is delayed and the gap between supply and potential demand diminishes due to growing demand for energy and falling supply (caused by expected decline of the capital stock if it is not replaced in time).

In fact, reform of natural monopolies, and of the electricity sector in particular, should be considered as one of the tools of structural policy, stimulating efforts to increase production efficiency by adding further pressure for restructuring.

Another problem in the current Russian economy is the widening gap between producer and consumer prices. In October 2000 producer prices increased 28.8 per cent relative to December 1999, while consumer prices increased by only 16.5 per cent. Given that the gap between producer and consumer prices was already quite substantial in 1999 (producer prices increased 67 per cent, while consumer prices grew 36.5 per cent), it is possible that the Russian economy is accumulating inflationary potential. It is expected that this gap may grow in the medium term since more rapid growth of domestic energy prices is expected in case of natural monopolies restructuring. This may mean a slowdown in economic growth if no substantial cost reduction and increase of production efficiency occur.

ECONOMIC POLICY: THE NEAR TERM

The 2002–4 macroeconomic policy programme and President Putin's annual address to the Federal Assembly on 3 April 2001 provided focal points for an evolving discussion on budget and debt policy. The core point of the discussion is strengthening of reform, constructive behaviour towards international financial markets, as well as improving the situation for private market bonds maturing in the 2002–4 period (e.g. MinFin 4).

A strategic direction in budget and debt policy is starting to emerge – to make the fiscal process more transparent and forward-looking, to adopt a programme of debt management reform, and to prepare fiscal policy more rigorously for the eventuality of future external shocks and handling of the 2003 debt-service peak.[33] In other words, Russian economic policymakers are already actively and formally considering fiscal, macro and debt policies for the period up to and including 2004, based on conservative assumptions and the need to avoid pro-cyclical fiscal action and the need to sustain fiscal restructuring.[34] This is clearly an encouraging sign. This development includes continuing the credit upgrade momentum and securing private market access in terms of future refinancing, while being cautious about adding to the existing stock of debt.

> **66The Duma would have the right to either approve or reject the first, current, budget, but not to change its parameters99**

President Putin's annual address on 3 April 2001 and the subsequent annual budget address focused among other things on fiscal and budget policies. As such, this represented a continuation of a more general discussion among Russian economic policymakers. Putin has directly proposed construction of future annual budgets in two parts, one current and one for future needs, with the latter intended as an insurance mechanism against external shocks and debt-service peaks. The second part of the budget would be built using revenues generated by an advantageous economic conjuncture, both external and domestic.[35] Specifically, Putin proposes a new mechanism of approving the annual budget. The Duma would have the right to either approve or reject the first, current, budget, but not to change its parameters (i.e. not to argue with the government's assessment of the potential for excess budget revenues). Currently the Duma loses this right only after the first reading of the budget draft. As regards the second part of the budget, the government would have more room for manoeuvre in terms of introducing changes and amendments along the way.[36]

This Putin proposal should be taken as a political confirmation of ideas already raised in the Russian policy debate. Leading government members have already proposed preparing the necessary amendments to the

Budget Code in order to implement the idea, expressed by Putin. In practical terms the position is this: while not ruling out diplomatic consultations on the possibility of a future Paris Club rescheduling deal covering the 2003 debt-service peak, Russia is no longer to assume such a deal as certain and should instead include in its policies the eventuality that Russia will handle all the debt payments on its own. This approach was further indirectly confirmed at the top-level Russian–German summit in St Petersburg in April 2001, where the German chancellor declared that Germany was ready to support a Russian debt restructuring effort in 2003–4 if the economic situation at that time deteriorated so as to make such an effort necessary.

The 2002 and 2003 budgets might therefore be constructed on the basis of full Paris Club payments, without assumptions of external debt rescheduling or restructuring of payments originally due. Deputy Prime Minister/Minister of Finance Alexei Kudrin has already confirmed that the 2002 budget (to be deficit-free) will be drafted assuming full scheduled external debt payments. This has also been supported by leading Duma officials. For example Alexander Shokhin, chairman of the Duma Banking Committee, has welcomed this plan.

According to Kudrin, the government will pursue three main avenues in order to be able to handle even the debt-peak years: fiscal policy (formally balanced budgets with the likelihood of overall surpluses in practice), selective work with IFIs (the World Bank, and later the IMF), and private market access for refinancing of maturing bonds. As noted above, Russia would seek the understanding of, for example, Germany for sovereign debt rescheduling only if the economic situation deteriorated substantially by 2003. Thus, in addition to ordering preparation of the 2002 budget and macroeconomic forecasts for 2002, Prime Minister Kasyanov has mandated the Ministry of Finance and other relevant ministries to outline a financial plan up to and including 2004, as well as the necessary macroeconomic forecasts to accompany such a plan.[37] The government was preparing to discuss the main parameters of the 2002 budget in a cabinet session on 24 May, and the Ministry of Finance submitted the full 2002 budget to the government by 1 August.

There are two main reasons for this gradual shift to a more forward-looking fiscal policy and changed debt policy emphasis, one politico-economic, the other connected with foreign policy. On the former, the government is seeking a realistic 'insurance policy' against reliance on external factors. Also, it is keen to avoid the 2001 situation when a Paris Club rescheduling was budgeted but then did not appear, leading to time lost in Duma budget renegotiations. On the foreign policy perspective, the Kremlin appears to be tired of having to go to the G7/Paris Club every year with requests for debt relief – requests which are, in the current international political environment, less politically acceptable not only for the leading G7 countries but also for the Kremlin administration.

At the Palermo G7 Finance Ministers meeting, the G7 expressed satisfaction and confidence with the Russian government's policy of paying in full on its 2001 obligations, and with the package of budget amendments which has been approved by the Duma. The Russian delegation stressed that while the situation in 2001 might be manageable, Russia could be forced to come back to the Paris Club for consultations in the future, referring to the 2003 debt-service peak (see also the recent German comments on this issue, above). In bilateral talks, several G7 ministers expressed an understanding that this might be the case should the economic situation worsen. The Russian side also continues to refer to the June 1999 G7 Cologne communiqué, where a G7 commitment to the pursuit of a comprehensive deal on Russia's Paris Club debt was affirmed. (The exact words were: 'In order to support Russia's efforts towards macroeconomic stability and sustainable growth, we encourage the Paris Club to continue to deal with the problem of the Russian debt arising from Soviet-era obligations, aiming at comprehensive solutions at a later stage once Russia has established conditions that enable it to implement a more ambitious economic reform programme'.)

Relations with the IMF are another issue. During January–March 2001, the Russian position regarding the IMF underwent some change, mainly as a response to the IMF's unwillingness to begin consultations on a three-year programme. Instead of starting discussions on such a medium-term programme, the IMF basically offered Russia a 'two-stage' approach: first a one-year precautionary programme, then, later, discussions on a two-year programme (covering 2002–3, including the 2003 debt-service peak). Recently, a joint government–Central Bank memorandum on economic policies (with policies and targets as agreed with IMF missions) pertaining to a one-year precautionary programme was concluded and announced.[38] However, the Russian government has declared that it sees little reason to go through the full formal process for a mere one-year precautionary agreement.

Thus, Russia will not submit the memorandum on economic policies to the IMF board for a *formal* review and vote. Instead the memorandum will be circulated informally to the IMF and form the basis for a monitoring type of relationship over the next year. The Russian side justifies this by pointing out that discussions concern a one-year precautionary programme only (while Russia wanted consultations to begin on a medium-term programme) and that Russia is confident of being able to handle the situation alone during this period. The IMF has responded with understanding, and the Russian side has emphasized that co-operation with the IMF will continue during this period, with regular (half-year or more frequent) mission visits to evaluate progress under the soon-to-be-published memorandum on economic policies. This co-operation will continue with an eye to deciding at some later point on the possibility for initiating consultations on a medium-term, non-precautionary programme, covering 2002–3.

Separately, World Bank programmes continue, and there is a possibility that the board of the World Bank could approve three new Russian projects, totalling $280 million at the end of June. Existing World Bank projects planned for disbursement in the 2001 financial year amount to $600 million. At the same time, given the strong balance-of-payments situation, the fourth tranche of the structural adjustment loan is unlikely to be disbursed. Note that during April the Russian side in any case started to deal with the main IMF prior action of amending banking sector legislation (three bank restructuring amendments).[39]

Given all of the above, the Russian economic policy road map for the remainder of 2001 and the coming years is busy. Items on the very near-term agenda are dominated by Duma legislation relevant to economic policy, such as the business deregulatory reforms, further tax reforms, the judicial reforms and the Land Code. Specifically, the authorities were targeting approval of the following initiatives in the necessary three Duma votes and the one required Federation Council hearing by the start of the Duma summer recess in mid-July: the new profit tax (already approved in one reading), a new tax on natural resource extraction and excises, the three business de-regulatory/de-bureaucratization initiatives, banking sector reforms (third reading expected on 17 May), and a new law on combatting the flow of illegally acquired capital. The political decision on how to proceed with UES restructuring was, as noted, expected by May 16. In addition, the aim was to have at least some Duma readings of the new Land Code, of a new Labour Code and of a complex of pension reform initiatives completed by mid-July. The schedule for the Duma's autumn session was to conclude work on a new Customs Code.

Against this background, Prime Minister Kasyanov's comment that Russia would be a 'different country' should this agenda be fulfilled (and implemented we should add) is understandable. The government's ability to pursue these measures through the required readings will be another important test. In a similar vein, the Kremlin's willingness to sponsor these reforms with President Putin's political capital will be a related test – an indication of the Kremlin's political stamina and the kind of political trade-offs the Kremlin is ready to make as complex and not uncontroversial structural reforms are embarked upon. As already noted, positive signs include the passing of the new profit tax passing on 11 April of the new Arbitration-Process Code in the first reading, and the full approval of the 'IMF package' of amendments to banking sector reforms.

Notes

[1] Any views and analyses expressed in this chapter should not be assigned to a specific institution to which the authors are affiliated.

[2] See, for example, Mau Vladimir (2000), 'Strategiya razvitiya i ee mesto v noveyshey rossiiskoy istorii', Itogi, No.21, and Yasin Evgeny 'Novaya epokha, starye trevogi – vzglyad liberala na razvitie Rossii', Fond Liberalnaya missiya. See also the interesting discussion on the burst of reforms in 1992, the subsequent 'semi-equilibrium' of reforms between late 1993 and 1998, and the new agenda for reforms from 2000 in Gaidar Yegor (2000) 'The struggle for a free economy and society in Russia', The Sir Ronald Trotter Lecture, New Zealand Business Roundtable.

[3]The concept of the investment climate as understood in the new Russian economic strategy and programme drafted in early 2000 is similar to the concept outlined and discussed by Stern Nicholas, the World Bank Chief Economist, in Stern Nicholas (2001), 'A strategy for development', ABCDE keynote address, May. For example, improving the investment climate is about policies and institutions which 'affect not just the level of capital investments but also the productivity of existing investments – indeed of all factors of production – and the willingness to make productive investments for the longer term' (Nicholas Stern, 'A strategy for development').

[4]Mau, Vladimir and Starodubrovskaya, Irina (2001), *The Challenge of Revolution*, Oxford University Press.

[5]See, for example, various reports from EEG, Ministerstvo finansov Rossiiskoy Federatsii, 'Obzor ekonomicheskikh pokazatelyey'.

[6]It should be stressed that as this chapter was concluded, Goskomstat, the Russian statistical agency, announced a significant alteration of nominal GDP figures over recent years, resulting in changes to real GDP growth numbers. for example, 1999 real GDP growth is now reported at 5.4 per cent rather than 3.2 per cent previously, and 2000 growth at 8.3 per cent, up from the previously reported 7.7 per cent.

[7]Similar results are also found in Belousov, A. and Ivanter, A. (2001) 'Konets stagnatsii', *Expert* magazine, 26 March. Andrei Belousov is head of the Centre or Macroeconomic Analysis and Short-Term Forecasting at the Russian Academy of Sciences, and part of the working group behind Russia's long-term economic strategy and medium-term economic action plan.

[8]See also the note on growth decomposition in 2000 by Frenkel, A. *et al.* (2001) 'Faktory rosta izmenilis', Vedomosti, April 18.

[9]This analysis is supported by the findings of the leading indicators index created by Tsentr Razvitia. See Razvitia Tsentr (2001), *Svodny operezhayushy indeks*, January (2001).

[10]This, of course, does not preclude the use of macroeconomic policies such as the establishment of a stabilisation fund as a way of managing volatile revenue flows from the resource sector, and policies to restrain the temptation of pro-cyclical fiscal policy by emphasizing the need to sustain the push for fiscal restructuring, both in terms of federal expenditures and regional fiscal sanitation. For a recent review of the experience and rationale behind 'stabilisation funds' in resource-rich economies experiencing windfall gains, see Everhart, Stephen and Duval-Hernandez, Robert (2001) 'Management of oil windfalls in Mexico: historical experience and policy options for the future', the World Bank/IFC, mimeo.

[11]As two of the leading contributors to the literature on exchange rate dynamics in transition and reforming economies put it: 'It is important to note, as a conclusion, that the Balassa-Samuelson effect is an equilibrium phenomenon, not an undesirable transitory effect that ought to be counteracted through policy actions … The real appreciation reflects the natural evolution of the economy which has to be translated into relative price changes.' See Halpern, L. and Wyplosz, C. (2001) 'Economic transformation and real exchange rates in the 2000s: the Balassa-Samuelson connection', March, mimeo. See also Halpern, L. and Wyplosz, C. (1998) 'Equilibrium exchange rates in transition economies: further results', November, mimeo.

[12]The most comprehensive studies in this regard are McKinsey (1999), 'Unlocking economic growth in Russia', October, and the World Bank (B. Pinto, V. Drebentsov, A. Morozov) (1999) 'Dismantling Russia's non-payments system: creating conditions for growth'.

[13]See also the encompassing analysis by Dynnikova, O. (2000) 'Makroekonomicheskie perspektivy ukrepleniya rublya I valyutnaya politika', EEG-Ministry of Finance, July.

[14]For example, in the long interview in *Literaturnaya Gazeta*, April 4–10, 2001.

[15]Indeed, given that Russia is a resource-rich economy, an emphasis on financial system restructuring and reform (as part of a broader push to improve the investment climate) is likely to be particularly important. For a recent analysis of the negative relationship between natural resource abundance and economic growth, with a focus on the role of the financial system, see Gylfason, Thorvaldur and Zoega, Gylfi 'Natural resources and economic growth: the role of investments', CEPR discussion papers, No. 2743. It is worth quoting their conclusion: 'We conclude that economic and structural reforms leading to more efficient capital markets, increased investment and a better allocation of capital across sectors may help start growth in countries that are well endowed in terms of natural resources. An excessive dependence on natural resources may, *ceteris paribus*, stifle the development of efficient capital markets. Even so, active measures to construct an institutional environment that contributes to saving and high-quality investment may ensure growth and enhance welfare in the presence of abundant natural resources.' This is likely to apply in particular to Russia, given the potential for major returns to scale due to the high-quality human capital endowment.

[16]The government may adjust the inflation expectation to 16 per cent from 12–14 per cent.

[17]The Ministry of Finance: 'Predvaritelnaya otsenko ispolneniya obyemov finansirovaniya raskhodov, defitsita I postupleniya dokhodov federalnovo byudzheta', January, February, March 2001.

[18]Note also that the recently initiated auctions of quotas on water resources (e.g. fishing rights) are doing very well, and revenues are significantly above expectations. For the first six such auctions in February and March, the government netted some R1.6 billion.

[19]For an analysis of and background to the long-term economic strategy and the 2000–1 macroeconomic action plan drafted and concluded during the first half of 2000, see Gavrilenkov, Yevgeny and Sundstrom, Niclas (2001) 'The Russian economy under President Putin: policy, challenges, prospects – a discussion', SMF-London to be published.

[20]On the slowdown or lull in the pursuit of economic reforms after the first half-year or so of the Putin regime, see also the insightful discussion by Professor Yegor Gaidar in *Literaturnaya Gazeta* (interview, 4–10 April 2001). See furthermore the outstanding treatise of the early part of Russian economic reforms by Yegor Gaidar in 'Renewal of Russian reforms', on 26 January 2001 (mimeo), as well as Gaidar Yegor (2000) 'The struggle for a free economy and society in Russia', the Sir Ronald Trotter Lecture, New Zealand.

[21]This was emphasized by President Putin himself in the major programmatic interview published in four Russian newspapers on 22 March 2001. See 'Vladimir Putin: za god ya stal dobre', *Izvestia*, 22 March 2001.

[22]The importance of the business reforms as an indication of the government's political ability to concentrate its efforts on a prioritized task and push it through is treated in Mau, Vladimir (2001) 'Deregulirovanie predprinimatelskoi deyatelnosti kak put postroeniya silnovo gosudarstvo', *Itogi*, 15 January, and 'Prostota protiv vorovstva', *Itogi*, 27 March.

[23]This work on credit rating analysis and on rating and spread relationship is directed by Christopher Kelly, Sovereign Credit Research, SSSB.

[24]See 'Vystuplenie Prezidenta Rossiiskoi Federatsii V.V. Putina na rasshirennom zasedanii kollegii Ministerstva finansov', 16 April 2001.

[25]For a full analysis of the challenge of structural fiscal reforms (mainly in the form of expenditure side restructuring), see the excellent paper by Alexander Ustinov, 'Vliyanie strukturnykh reform na byudzhet Rossiiskoy Federatsii v dolgosrochnoy perspektive', BEA-EEG-Ministry of Finance, 2000.

[26]Permanent capital outflows are an indicator of such 'openness'.

[27]Following, for instance, a decline in energy prices and currency inflows into Russia.

[28]This share may be higher if calculated at world market prices, but obviously it should be much less than half of GDP.

[29]See, for instance, Auty, Richard M. (2001) 'The political economy of resource-driven growth', *European Economic Review*, May, and Sachs, Jeffrey D. and Werner, Andrew M. 'The case of natural resources', mimeo (Russia was not examined in these papers).

[30]Real negative interest rates can also be viewed in the context of the high dollarization of the Russian economy, a signal of low credibility in government policies. Obviously, interest rates on dollar deposits are positive, and this is actually the benchmark for economic agents in Russia. In the context of ongoing appreciation of the rouble, real interest rates on rouble accounts are thus negative.

[31]Negative real interest rates could also be seen as a serious impediment to pension reform, since serious accumulation of funds is impossible in such an environment.

[32]The average price for 1 kWh was just over one cent in Russia in 2000.

[33]The main manifestations of this fiscal policy evolution are to be found in the following documents/presentations: Vladimir Putin, 'O byudzhetnoi politike na 2002 god, 2002', mimeo, Vladimir Putin, 'Vystuplenie Prezidenta Rossiiskoi Federatsii V.V. Putina na rasshirennom zasedanii kollegii Ministerstva finansov', 16 April 2001 and Aleksei Kudrin, 'Ob itogakh ispolneniya federalnovo byudzheta za 2000 god i zadachakh organov finansovoi sistemy Rossisskoi Federatsii na 2001 god i na srednesrochnyuyu perspektivy', Ministry of Finance, 16 April 2001. This evolution in fiscal policy is comprised of the following aspects: use of the most conservative macroeconomic assumptions possible, establishment of a stabilisation fund (or reserve budget), re-confirmation of the policy of a 'non-deficit budget', debt management reforms, further regional fiscal sanitation and expenditure restructuring and the next phase of tax reforms.

[34]The underlying macroeconomic assumptions, including one 'optimistic' and one 'pessimistic' scenario, as well as a forward-looking policy discussion, are to be found in the Ministry for Economic Development and Trade document, 'Proekt – Stsenarnye usloviya funktsionirovaniya ekonomiki v 2002 gody i na period do 2004 goda', 4 April 2001, mimeo.

[35]For a recent review of the experience and rationale behind 'stabilisation funds' in resource-rich economies experiencing windfall gains, see Everhart, Stephen and Duval-Hernandez, Robert 'Management of oil windfalls in Mexico: historical experience and policy options for the future', the World Bank/IFC, mimeo.

[36]Leading economic policy-relevant Duma officials have already expressed understanding and sympathy for this idea. The chairman of the Duma Banking Committee, Alexander Shokhin, has stated that the Duma will probably consider the 2002 budget based on these new principles.

[37]Postanovlenia pravitelstva, 3 April 2001, No. 428.

[38]See 'Zayavlenie pravitelstva Rossiiskoi Federatsii i Tsentralnovo Banka Rossiiskoi Federatsii ob ekonomicheskoi politike na 2001 god i nekotorykh aspektakh strategii ha srednesrochnhyu perspektivy', 13 April 2001.

[39]There are a few other minor prior actions, such as specifying the requirements for hiring an international consultant to carry out a review of Sberbank, outlining more clearly the strategy for exiting the CBR from its offshore subsidiaries (this process is already under way), and clearing final hurdles to allow the CBR to resume issuance of CBR bills as liquidity-regulating instruments.

12

RUSSIA: FINANCIAL MARKET PROSPECTS[1]

GOOHOON KWAN[2]

INTRODUCTION

RUSSIA APPEARS TO HAVE FULLY OVERCOME the August 1998 crisis, with its economic performance likely to be the best in the region in 2000. Growth of real GDP was at a historic high of 7.5 per cent in the first half of 2000, beating the market's initially cautious expectations that 1999 growth of 3.2 per cent would be short-lived. Most other key macro indicators also remained very strong, setting new historic records almost every month (See Table 12.1). The unemployment rate fell from a 1998 high of 13.3 per cent to 9.8 per cent in mid-2000. Current and fiscal accounts are also expected to register record performance in 2000, with the trade surplus through August reaching $39 billion (or some 25 per cent of GDP) and the federal budget registering a surplus of 3.5 per cent of GDP during the same period. On the back of strong external perform-ance and tight fiscal policy, international reserves more than doubled to a historic high of about $26 billion in October compared with a year earlier, despite still sizeable capital outflow and tiny private and public capital inflow. There are increasing signs that a decade of wrenching economic contraction is indeed over, with Russia entering a virtuous circle of a strong budget, remagnetization and economic growth, although the country cannot be immune to cyclical swings.

Table 12.1 *Key macroeconomic indicators*

	1996	1997	1998	1999	2000F	2001F
Real GDP (% change)	–3.6	0.9	–4.9	3.2	6.5	4.5
Inflation (Dec–Dec)	21.8	11	84.4	36.5	19	13
Trade surplus (% of GDP)	5.5	4.0	6.4	19.5	23.9	14.0
Federal budget deficit/GDP (%)	9.0	7.4	6.3	1.3	–1.8	–0.5
Urals blend oil price ($/bl avg.)	20.1	18.3	11.8	17.1	26.8	22.5
Real effective R/$ exchange rate *	100	107	89	65	74	81

Sources: Central Bank of Russia, Finance Ministry, Goskomstat, Bloomberg, ABN AMRO forecasts

*1996 = 100

Despite these benign economic developments, risks for investors definitely remain high. Russia still relies heavily on export of commodities, which represent as much as 70–80 per cent of total exports, with oil and gas alone representing 40–50 per cent. Russia would thus be vulnerable to a sharp global economic downturn as its external and fiscal balances would be hurt by weak commodity prices, although the country would be in a far better position to deal with such external shocks than before. Also, its external debt burden remains high, with federal debt standing at about 85 per cent of GDP in 1999, requiring at least one more round of debt relief from Soviet-debt holders. Russia's relations with the West, particularly the US, which are important for rebuilding the economy, remain vulnerable to unstable political moods and other unpredictable geopolitical factors.

> **"post-crisis economic and political developments provide a potential turning point in the development of Russia's financial markets"**

This chapter reviews the latest financial market developments in Russia and discusses their short and medium-term outlook, focusing on the role of post-crisis economic and political developments. Clearly it is very difficult to make forecasts for Russian financial markets in the medium perspective, since major factors affecting them are largely external and difficult to control or counteract. Furthermore, Russian markets are of an embryonic and fluid nature, reflecting the legacy of Soviet-era planning and slow financial sector reforms. Nonetheless, post-crisis economic and political developments provide a potential turning point in the development of Russia's financial markets, warranting a fresh look at the potential, which has been completely off the screens of most investors.

PRE-CRISIS: VICIOUS CIRCLE

The Russian economy suffered heavily for a decade from a vicious circle of demonetization, crowding out and output decline. After the break-up of the Soviet Union in 1991, Russia's public finances became a shambles as the country inherited the Soviet legacy of heavy spending obligations that were far too large to be covered by falling revenues. The fiscal situation was made worse by a declining economy. With sharp spending cuts largely ruled out by a Communist-controlled parliament, the government had to borrow heavily to meet its spending needs, initially from the Central Bank and later from the securities markets, charging a high inflation tax, crowding out financial resources from the economy and thereby choking off producers. The economy reacted by relying increasingly on non-rouble instruments such as barter, inter-enterprise credits and the US dollar, which were difficult to tax or even monitor.

This demonetization process widened the fiscal financing gap further by eroding the tax base which, in a vicious circle, induced further demonetization. While this vicious circle could arise in any country with a large and sustained budget deficit, the degree of Russia's demonetization was extreme as a result of its small and fragile financial sector and major transition shocks associated with the break-up of the Soviet Union. On average, Russia had a budget deficit of 6.5 per cent of GDP between 1994 and 1998, which was equivalent to about 45 per cent of broad money (see Table 12.2). The deficit-money ratio, which indicates the extent of crowding out, was much lower in other countries in the region with large budget deficits in the same period, including Turkey, Romania and Hungary (see Figure 12.1).

Table 12.2 *Selected fiscal and other macro indicators*

	1994	1995	1996	1997	1998	1999	2000F
Inflation (Dec–Dec, %)	215.1	131.3	21.8	11.0	84.4	36.5	19.2
Real GDP (% change)	–12.6	–4.1	–3.6	0.9	–4.9	3.2	6.5
Fed deficit/GDP (%)	11.4	5.4	9.0	7.4	6.3	1.3	–1.8
Fed revenue (CPI deflated)	115	109	100	101	73	84	117
Fed non-interest spending (CPI deflated)	173	107	100	101	69	59	67
Rouble M2/GDP (%)	15.9	13.6	13.0	14.2	16.7	15.5	17.4
Fed deficit/rouble M2 (%)	72	40	69	52	38	8	–10

Sources: Central Bank of Russia, Finance Ministry, Goskomstat, Bloomberg, ABN AMRO forecast

Figure 12.1 *Budget deficit and broad money (as % of GDP, average for 1994–8)*

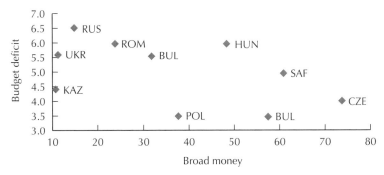

Source: Statistical agencies of national authorities

CHANGING PARADIGMS: VIRTUOUS CIRCLE OF TWIN SURPLUSES

Environments in the Russian financial markets have changed dramatically since the economic crisis of August 1998. Two macroeconomic events are particularly important: an extremely large trade surplus and an unprecedented fiscal surplus. Thanks to strong commodity prices and the cheap rouble, huge export proceeds were brought in and converted into roubles, increasing reserve money 75 per cent year-on-year in August 2000. This huge liquidity injection from the large trade surplus could have been taken away as before by the government or eroded rapidly through inflation if the budget had remained in a large deficit and continued to borrow massively from the banking system. In the event, supported by high oil prices and conservative fiscal policy, the budgetary stance dramatically improved in 1999 and is expected to show a surplus in 2000 – unprecedented phenomena for this deficit-ridden country. More importantly, there is strong evidence that the twin surpluses could be sustained beyond 2000. High oil prices are expected to be temporary, but the fiscal conservatism appears to be firmly embedded in the economic reform strategies of the new government as a strong safeguard against the lax fiscal policy of the previous regime. Similarly, commodity prices will enter into a cyclical downturn in the future but the rouble is likely to remain competitive and help sustain the trade surplus given the sharp initial depreciation of 75 per cent and ongoing smooth remonetization as discussed below.

The twin surpluses have broken the decade-old vicious circle of demonetization, budget deficit and recession. With no funding demand from the government, the ample liquidity is finding its way towards producers, albeit with lags and leaks. Lending competition, which is still at an embryonic stage, is likely to pick up soon, led by aggressive Russian banks. There are already signs that corporate lending has begun to increase, albeit gradually and at a short tenor. In the first half of 2000, banks increased their corporate lending by 20 per cent relative to the end of last year or about $4 billion, including an estimated $1.2 billion from the state savings bank (Sberbank), compared with virtually no change in the same period last year (see Figure 12.2). The reliance on barter and inter-enterprise credit appears to remain high but is declining sharply. The payables of industrial, construction, transportation and agricultural companies have fallen from a pre-crisis peak of 18 months of industrial output to about nine months. Their receivables have also halved from a pre-crisis peak of 12 months of industrial output. Reflecting improved corporate cashflows, overdue receivables fell to a six-year low of 40 per cent of total receivables by July 2000, down from the pre-crisis level of 53 per cent.

Despite the large liquidity injection, overall domestic credit remained roughly unchanged due to the budget surplus, helping to limit inflation (see Figure 12.3). Domestic credit in the banking system remained virtually flat through August 2000, as money supply was almost fully

Figure 12.2 *Domestic credits*

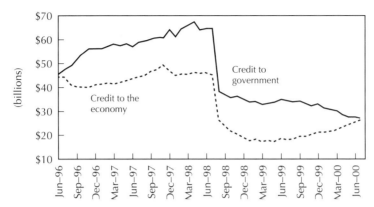

Source: Central Bank of Russia

Figure 12.3 *Credit and money supply*

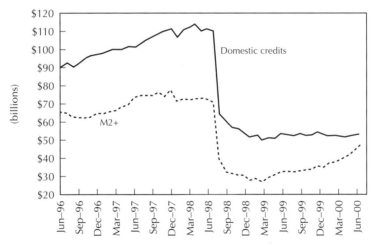

Source: Central Bank of Russia

funded by the accumulation of foreign assets. Indeed, inflation for the first eight months of 2000 was limited to 12.7 per cent, compared with a 36–41 per cent surge in money supply over the same period. For all practical purposes, this macroeconomic environment is very similar to what is seen under a currency-board arrangement, where money grows only through accumulation of reserves rather than through injections of credit, reflecting growing money demand. Transaction demand for the rouble also appears to be increasing thanks to strong political commitment to collecting taxes in cash and barring in-kind payments, especially between the public utilities and their customers. Indeed, despite a year-on-year increase in rouble M2 of some 60 per cent, the change in money supply, if measured in months of industrial production or federal revenue collection, was minor.

The benign mix of large trade and fiscal surpluses continues to spur economic growth. Real GDP, which posted record year-on-year growth of 7.5 per cent in H1 2000, is expected to grow 6.5–7 per cent for the full year, driven mainly by companies involved in exporting and import substitution. Preliminary earnings data suggest that the declared pre-tax earnings of large and medium-sized enterprises, a significant part of which are expected to be invested in the economy, increased to about $23 billion in the first seven months of 2000 compared with $14 billion in the same period in 1999. These aggregate profits would be even higher if unreported earnings (or illegal capital flight) were included.

Growth in 2001 is likely to slow down but remain strong by Russian standards, driven by robust investment and domestic demand. Investment is likely to be funded largely from retained corporate earnings, following the pattern of 2000. In the first half of 2000, 53 per cent of investment, which surged 17.2 per cent year-on-year, was financed by retained earnings, 24 per cent by budgetary funds, and only 4 per cent by bank lending. In addition, non-fuel commodity producers, which account for about 30 per cent of exports, are likely to benefit from strong global demand, which could increase non-fuel commodity prices by 4.5 per cent in 2001 according to the latest IMF forecast, up from 3.2 per cent in 2000. By attracting foreign capital and reversing capital flight, the economy could continue to grow at a rate similar to that seen in 2000. This would, however, depend on sweeping corporate and banking reforms.

RUSSIAN FINANCIAL MARKETS AND THEIR PROSPECTS

Money and credit markets

The twin surpluses both pose challenges and offer opportunities to players in Russia's money markets. The effect of remonetization is most evident in the liquidity situation of the banking system. On the one hand, banks are flush with cash brought into the country by exports. Meanwhile, banks' historical sources of easy profits are rapidly disappearing, with the currency stabilising and the government turning from a heavy borrower into a net lender. We estimate that commercial banks kept as much as $10 billion worth of roubles at the Central Bank at zero or close-to-zero interest rates at the end of July 2000. This represents roughly 15 per cent of commercial banks' aggregate assets, compared with 10 per cent in December 1999 and 7 per cent in December 1998. This surge in liquidity despite a sharp rise in corporate lending suggests a structural imbalance between rising deposits and increasing yet relatively lagging lending, as illustrated by a declining loans-to-deposits ratio. The ratio fell to 1.15x in July 2000, down from 1.3x a year earlier and 1.4x two years previously (see Figure 12.4).

"corporate demand for longer-term financing is increasing rapidly along with the improving perceived growth outlook"

An immediate challenge from the impact of the changing banking environment is an acute tenor mismatch. Bank liability remains very short-term, with about 60 per cent of corporate deposits at a tenor of less than three months and 90 per cent of household deposits at less than six months. By contrast, corporate demand for longer-term financing is increasing rapidly along with the improving perceived growth outlook, with some local and multinational firms adopting aggressive investment and expansion strategies for the next year. As a result, the money-market yield curve is very steep, with the spread between one-year and one-month money as high as 12–13 percentage points. Credit markets remain very thin and illiquid with no fresh issuance of benchmark government notes, although the longer end of the yield curve has tightened considerably as prices and exchange rates are stabilized.

Figure 12.4 *Loans to deposits ratio (x)*

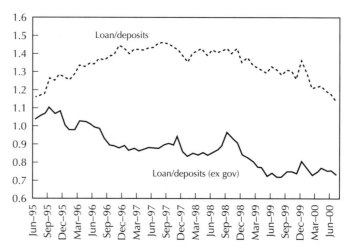

Source: Central Bank of Russia

Despite the drawbacks in the Russian money and credit markets, the net short-term impact of the twin surpluses is largely positive. First, corporate lending is unlikely to be as risky as before since corporate financial positions have drastically improved thanks to the sharp devaluation and ongoing economic recovery. Also, corporate lending is expected to provide a more steady and diversified source of profits compared with the pre-crisis government lending, which was extremely profitable ex-ante but highly vulnerable to political risks. Second, short-term money has become an increasingly stable source of longer-term funding as overall liquidity in the economy has improved and perceived credit risks have declined along with sustained stability in currency and prices. Third, both borrowers and lenders appear to be actively seeking ways to lengthen their loan maturities. EBRD and World Bank loans are one way of achieving this, and have already created competition among potential local joint lenders, who want to co-finance profitable businesses at reduced risk. The EBRD is already active in financing investment projects in Russia, with fresh loans expected to reach about $630 million this year compared with last year's $220 million. The issuance of corporate notes (including promissory notes and medium-term notes) could offer other ways for large companies and banks to lengthen their loan maturities.

The medium-term outlook depends critically on the success of structural reforms. The government's medium-term economic programme intends to achieve high and sustainable economic growth through macro stabilisation and ambitious structural reforms. The programme details several explicit financial sector reform measures, which aim mostly to establish and improve the sector's legal basis. For example, the programme envisages the passage of laws on investment funds and investment accounts by Q1 2001 and a law on certificates of deposits by the end of 2001. The programme also plans to separate trust and proprietary accounts, introduce liberal tax treatment of investment losses, specify loss carry-over provisions, and simplify registration rules for corporate note issuance. Further measures will include introducing tax benefits for financial investments depending on the size and horizon of the investments. Elimination of tax on securities transactions, which has hindered the development of the securities market, is also on the agenda (see Figure 12.5). Even more important pushes are likely to come from broader structural measures aimed at addressing non-payments, murky corporate governance, inadequate bankruptcy and foreclosure procedures, and poor protection of minority shareholder rights.

Assuming that the ambitious reforms will be broadly on track, we expect Russian financial markets to grow faster than other sectors of the economy. Our sanguine expectation is based on widely established empirical evidence.[3] In an exercise to get broad guidance on the magnitude of long-term financial deepening in Russia, we took broad

Figure 12.5 *Yield curve of Russian government securities**

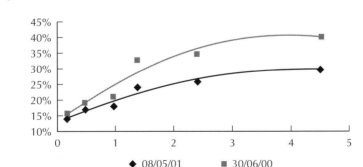

Source: Reuters
* Yields are indicative due to illiquidity of the government securities market

money-to-GDP ratios for 1995 in 166 countries as a proxy for financial depth. We also took per-capita income in US dollars for the same year as a proxy for the stage of economic development. A simple cross-country regression based on these data shows that an increase in the money-to-GDP ratio by about 2 percentage points is associated with an increase in per-capita income of $1000 (see Figure 12.6) although the degree of the strength depends on model specification.[4]

Based on the government economic programme, which envisages growth of per-capita GDP to $3500 by 2010 from the current level of $1400, we estimate that the money-to-GDP ratio could go up from the current 17 per cent to at least 21–22 per cent by 2010. This financial deepening would proceed even faster if structural reforms and macro stabilisation remain in force in the medium term. Russia's GDP measured according to purchasing power parity is far larger than its GDP measured by the market exchange rates (about five times larger using IMF methodology), reflecting reduced but still sizeable domestic price distortions (especially energy) and currency undervaluation. Furthermore, the large number of inter-enterprise credits, which stand at a sizeable 40 per cent of GDP even after a sharp decline from 57 per cent of GDP at end-1998, is expected to contribute to financial market deepening when and if they are securitized as in other advanced emerging-market countries.

Figure 12.6 *Level of economic development and financial deepening*

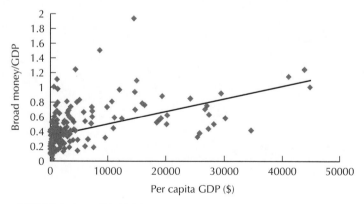

Source: IMF WEO database, ABN AMRO

External debt markets

Russia's external sovereign debt was a top performer in the emerging-market debt league in 2000, with a whopping 41 per cent gain for the first ten months of the year measured by the EMBI+ total return index for Russia. The external debt is likely to benefit further from the twin surpluses, which we expect to be firmly in place at least throughout 2001. On the back of a record high trade surplus and healthy fiscal surplus, the federal government's external debt service obligation for the next two years appears to be fully manageable, even without any fresh commercial borrowing (see Figure 12.7). The total annual external debt-service burden of around $13–14 billion (including some $4 billion of Paris Club debt service) could become onerous if the external environment should deteriorate sharply. However, for the rainy days, Russia appears to have two important safety nets in addition to orthodox fiscal measures. First, Russia could tap IMF support under a precautionary standby arrangement, which the two parties are expected to launch this year or early next year. Russia could also seek debt rescheduling from Paris Club creditors, who in principle agreed to consider such a possibility. Indeed, there are increasing signs that a temporary, two-year debt relief is in the pipeline, with further relief

Figure 12.7 *Emerging market debt performance*

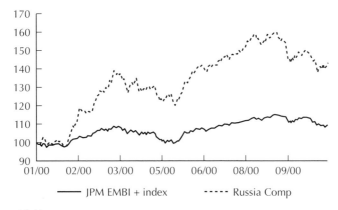

Source: J.P. Morgan

depending on balance of payments developments beyond 2002 and policy efforts by the Russian government.

We do not expect Russian eurobonds to be suppressed by new issuance down the road. For 2001, Russia has not excluded the possibility of tapping international markets to refinance the Russia 2001 eurobond maturity of $1 billion, as indicated by an ambiguous stance on this possibility in the 2001 budget. However, the government is unlikely to consider issuing eurobonds in 2001 unless market conditions are clearly in favour of Russia. In any case, the 2001 budget does not carry a significant risk of missing the zero-deficit target, even with lower world oil prices, since it is based on fairly conservative macroeconomic and global assumptions. Second, as a matter of principle, the new reformist government has strong reservations about commercial borrowing, due partly to significant cost implications and the painful stigma of the sovereign default under the previous government. In the worst-case scenario, Russia could use some of its accumulated international reserves as it did in 1999. These reserves stand at a record high of $25 billion, or about six months of imports. It is too early to talk about external borrowing needs for 2002 but the situation is unlikely to change materially given a relatively low debt-servicing burden in that year and the strong and credible commitment of the new government to a lean and balanced budget.

> **66for the rainy days, Russia appears to have two important safety nets in addition to orthodox fiscal measures.99**

The year 2003 does appear to pose a challenge, although it is much less serious than the one that Russia faced in 1998. The external debt service burden of the federal government peaks at $18 billion in 2003 (including the $3.5 billion MinFin 4 redemption), as shown in Figure 12.8. If there are no breakthroughs in Paris Club debt talks in the meantime, Russia might seek to extend the maturity of the MinFin 4 in line with previous restructuring of the MinFin 3, as the MinFin 4 has been declared junior debt due to its Soviet-era origins. In that context, the MinFin 4 appears to be the most risky federal debt despite repeated remarks by senior Finance Ministry officials claiming otherwise. However, even if MinFin 4 is restructured, the damage is unlikely to

Figure 12.8 *External debt service to private creditors and the IMF 2000–30*

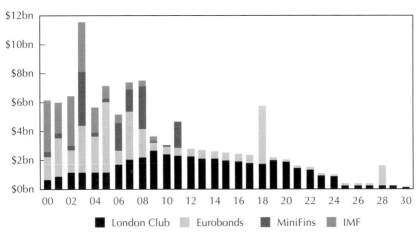

Source: IMF and Ministry of Finance

spread beyond MinFin 4 and MinFin 5, which are the only remaining Soviet-era obligations to private creditors. Such a risk has already been priced in and the restructuring measure is strictly in line with stated and implemented debt servicing policy of the Russian government.

The overall sovereign debt outlook also appears to be positive in the medium term. First, the new government is credibly committed to fiscal conservatism with the strong support of President Putin, as evidenced by the passage of a balanced 2001 budget in major readings by the state Duma in October 2000. Second, the chronic problem of federal expenditure control seems to be being resolved with the establishment of the federal treasury and the pursuit of ambitious regional reforms. Third, even with lower oil prices the government could collect suffi-cient, albeit declining revenues from the economy, since the country is unlikely to fall again into a contraction trap and the ongoing tax reforms are expected to provide a stable source of revenues.

If a conservative fiscal policy prevails against a reasonably favourable economic backdrop, we expect that the federal debt-to-GDP ratio will fall significantly in the next four years from 96 per cent to about 50 per cent (see Figure 12.9). Our baseline scenario assumes a small budget deficit of below 1 per cent of GDP during the next four years and a

Figure 12.9 *Federal debt-to-GDP ratio*

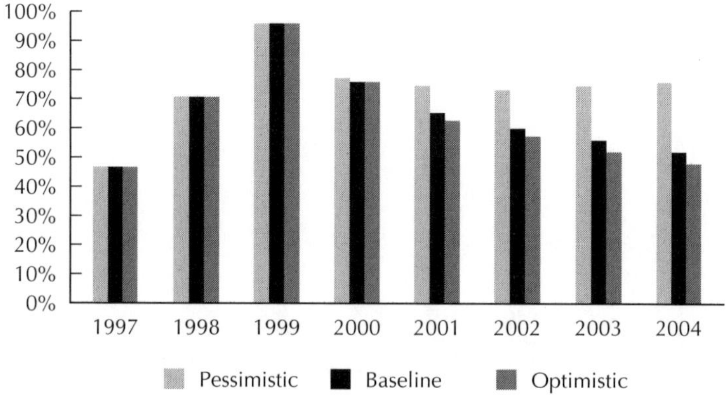

Source: Ministry of Finance and ABN AMRO forecast

gradual strengthening of the currency in real terms. In an alternative, reasonably pessimistic scenario where the debt-to-GDP ratio stays high due to macroeconomic instability, the deficit is assumed to be between 2 per cent and 3 per cent of GDP and the currency to remain weak. In a modestly optimistic scenario the deficit remains low but the currency is assumed to strengthen even faster than in the baseline scenario.

Equity market

The local equity market continues to depend heavily on external factors although daily moves of individual stocks are also affected occasionally by company-specific issues, notably corporate governance and share-holder rights. Figure 12.10 shows that the Russian equity market is far more strongly correlated with US equity markets than three other large emerging stock markets in the region – Turkey, Poland and Hungary. The latest averages of the 50-day rolling correlation between Russia and the Dow Jones Industrial Average were 0.79 compared with –0.36 for Turkey, 0.07 for Poland, and 0.00 for Hungary.

We identify two major reasons for this. The first is that the local investor pool is thin and their horizon is very short-term, largely due to weak and underdeveloped domestic financial markets. This underdevelop-ment transmits external volatility directly to the local equity market, which is thus held back despite significantly improved fundamentals.

Figure 12.10 *Stock markets – 50-day correlation with the Dow Jones Index (1 August– 23 October 2000)*

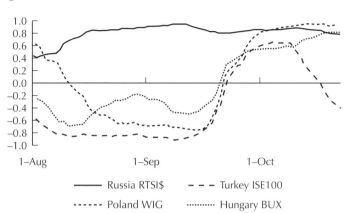

Source: Bloomberg
*Dow Jones with one-day lag to account for time differences

As noted in the previous section, banks are unlikely to be major players in the equity market as they are still undergoing a slow rehabilitation, with their balance sheets weak, small and highly constrained by short-term liabilities. Non-banking financial institutions including mutual funds, insurance companies and pension funds are in their infancy, with few sizeable institutions established. Mutual funds are unlikely to be major players in the near term although they are increasing efforts to tap household savings. The concept of mutual funds is fairly foreign to most households and, despite a high charge ratio of over 5 per cent, the profit margin is severely limited given the small size of per-account investments. The state pension fund, which is likely to register an unprecedented surplus of as much as 3 per cent of GDP this year, is the only sizeable potential non-banking player in the equity market. However, the room for sustained saving by the pension system is slim since pension reforms are unlikely to start in earnest until mid-2002. Corporate treasuries and sophisticated local private investors still seem to prefer offshore investment vehicles and their own pocket banks rather than the stock market for liquidity and asset management.

The second reason that the Russian equity market is highly vulnerable to external factors is that Russian sovereign risk in its broad sense (including political and policy risks) remains a dominant factor affecting the value of stocks, with sovereign spread still hovering at 850–1100bps over US treasuries. A dividend discount model suggests that a sustainable drop of 100bps in the sovereign spread will help increase the net present value of the stock market index by as much as 5 per cent given that the current discount rate is very high (see Table 12.3). The correlation of the RTS equity index with the EMBI+ Russian bond index is indeed markedly higher than in other major emerging markets such as Turkey and Poland. Average 50-day rolling correlation of stock market indices and sovereign EMBI bond indices was 0.90 for Russia in October 2000, compared with –0.14 for the Turkish ISE-100 and –0.39 for Poland (see Figure 12.12). The RTS's correlation with the Russian bond index was also stronger than its correlation with the Dow Jones (0.79).

Looking forward, we expect that the sovereign risk factor will lessen considerably in the near future. Moody's has indicated that it might upgrade Russian sovereign credit from B3 to B2 (the current level of Bulgaria and Venezuela) by putting Russia on a positive credit watch list in late August 2000. The perceived sovereign risk is also likely to fall with the start of reform programmes supported by the IMF and the World Bank. If the sovereign spread tightens to 600–800bps, which is comparable with other emerging markets, company-specific issues such as earnings, governance and shareholder rights are likely to gain more importance.

Figure 12.11 *Relation between the equity index and the sovereign risk premium*

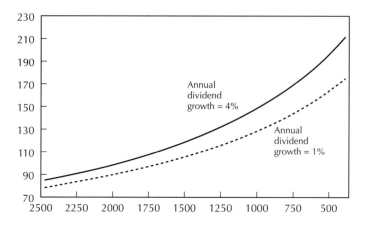

Table 12.3 *Application of a simple dividend discount model to Russia*

	Hypothetical equity index	Dividend *	Time discount	Sov. risk premium **	Risk-free rate***	Equity risk ****	Dividend growth
A year ago	20.0	1000	54.1	40.0	6.09	8.0	4.0
Base line	47.6	1000	25.1	11.0	6.09	8.0	4.0
End-Sept, 2000	50.0	1000	24.1	10.0	6.09	8.0	4.0
End-2000	57.1	1000	21.6	7.0	6.59	8.0	4.0
% Change							
Now versus a year ago	150	0.0	−55.6	−75.2	0.0	0.0	0.0
Now versus the base line	5	0.0	−4.0	−9.1	0.0	0.0	0.0
End-2000 versus end-Sept	14	0.0	−10.3	−29.9	8.2	0.0	0.0

* Arbitrary figure, which does not affect the relative value.

** Russia EMBI+ spread in percentages.

*** US 10-year Treasury bond at the time of writing.

**** Assumption based on consensus equity risk premium estimates of 3–8 per cent in core markets.

Figure 12.12 *50-day correlation with sovereign EMBI bond indices (1 August – 23 October 2000)*

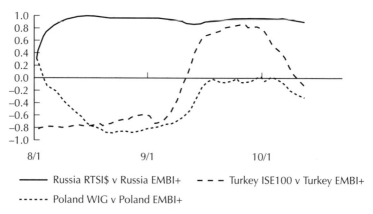

Source: Bloomberg

CONCLUSION

Russia's financial markets are clearly among the most underdeveloped of the various markets in Russia as well as in the region. However, post-crisis economic developments, notably the twin surpluses, appear to have reversed the underlying causes of the underdevelopment, probably in a sustainable manner. In that sense, Russian financial markets could become major beneficiaries of an ongoing reform drive and sustained macroeconomic stability. The development of local financial markets would in turn help to lengthen investment horizons, sharply reduce the country-risk premium, facilitate corporate funding, and promote economic growth. Needless to say, this turnaround will be possible only if the government stays on its declared course of liberal economic reforms.

Notes

[1] This article was written in October 2000.

[2] Any views and analyses expressed in this chapter should not be assigned to a specific institution to which the author is affiliated.

[3]See Goldsmith, Raymond William (1969) *Financial Structure and Development*, and King, Robert G. and Levine, Ross (1993) 'Finance and growth: Shumpeter might be right', *QJE*, August.

[4]This empirical relationship appears to be also robust under different specifications, including multivariate regressions based on average income levels between 1970 and 1995 and initial income levels in 1970 as independent variables.

13

CONCLUSIONS: HALF EMPTY OR HALF FULL?

PETER WESTIN

THE AUGUST 1998 CRISIS, in many ways, has proved a blessing in disguise for Russia. First, it dismissed the illusion that the economy was on the right track, an illusion created by an overvalued exchange rate, which relied on inflows of capital to high yields on government securities. Second, the crisis exposed the weakness of Russia's institutions, companies and banks (most of them hardly deserved the name), for which 'restructuring' was nothing more than a 13-letter word. Devaluation gave much of the Russian economy a new lease of life by making it competitive. However, the post-crisis economic and legal environment for economic agents, both domestic and foreign, remains highly unsatisfactory. Russia must use the opportunity to speed up structural and institutional reform, and thus to attract the investments, it desperately needs.

THE CRISIS AND THE ACHIEVEMENTS

The real sector

Russia's manufacturing suffered a series of devastating blows in the years before the 1998 crisis. First, Soviet manufacturing, which was largely dependent on state orders, was hit by a fall in demand from its main customer as state funds were depleted from the mid-1980s onwards. Russia's population of 147 million suffered a decline in their real income as market reforms were implemented, thus further depressing domestic demand for manufactured goods. The break-up of the Soviet Union and increased foreign presence meant that Russian manufacturing suddenly faced a new economic reality: competition. In addition, Russia had its own version of the phenomenon known as Dutch disease.[1] Economic dependence on exports of energy, minerals and metals helped to push up the real exchange rate, benefiting non-tradables but crowding out the manufacturing industry. The decline was only halted by the August 1998 devaluation, which gave domestic companies a new competitive edge. The effect of devaluation was particularly noticeable for import-competing sectors, as imports fell 50 per cent.

With the government after the crisis doing as much as possible to do as little as possible, it was encouraging to observe how Russian companies responded to the new environment. They seized the opportunity offered by devaluation, and sectors such as textiles, previously crushed by foreign competition due to the excessively strong rouble, rose like a phoenix from the ashes: a victory for market forces indeed.

The fiscal sphere

Prior to the crisis Russia had been struggling for more than a decade with an inability to collect taxes.[2] At the same time, fiscal spending was out of control. Shortly after the crisis tax collection started to improve. The combination of improved company profitability and increased pressure from the authorities for tax payment on time and in cash (particularly by large tax payers) led to a sudden increase in federal revenues. Also, the OPEC agreement in April 1999 led to an increase in world oil prices, providing another source of tax revenues from now more profitable Russian oil companies. In fact, tax collection since 1999 has exceeded targets set by the budget law. Furthermore, the government has curbed its spending habits. The budget law for 2001 requires a balanced budget, and the first draft of the 2002 budget predicts a federal surplus for the first time in the short history of post-Soviet Russia.

The virtual economy

In the early reform years lack of liquidity and financing quickly spawned the widespread phenomenon of non-payments and barter in Russian industry, creating what became known as 'the virtual economy' or 'the non-cash economy'. Enterprises did not pay for deliveries, and supplier companies survived by doing the same. Inter-enterprise arrears rapidly became a prodigious reality of the Russian economy. Furthermore, enterprises created a system of barter transactions. Just before the August 1998 crisis the share of barter in industrial sales stood at 52 per cent.

In the same way, both state and private companies stopped paying their workers, or paid salaries in kind. For the government this was one way of restricting budget spending, but there was also indictation that unpaid wage funds were used for speculation on the high-yield GKO market.[3]

❝In the early reform years lack of liquidity and financing quickly spawned the widespread phenomenon of non-payments and barter in Russian industry❞

After the crisis, pressure on companies to pay their taxes in cash forced them to increase pressure on each other to honour obligations in monetary form. The government set a good example by starting to pay off wage arrears to state employees and to reduce pension arrears. As a result of these processes non-payments and barter have declined significantly. The government is now meeting its obligations to workers and pensioners on time. In the private sector, wage arrears and the level of barter as a share of sales have fallen, standing at 17 per cent. Thus, the virtual economy, although not gone, has begun to shrink.

The oligarchs

The 1998 crisis also revealed the weakness of Russia's banking system, and the banking collapse hurt some of the most powerful individuals in Russia: the so-called 'oligarchs'. These business heavyweights, who previously played a major role in Russian politics, suddenly saw their influence weaken. President Putin has even demanded their complete withdrawal from the political arena. This is a move in the right direction, but it is likely to be a selective process. The oligarchs seem to be getting different treatment depending on their relationship with and attitude towards the Kremlin. This connects with a worrying aspect of Putin's Russia – infringement of freedom of speech. Powerful individuals who have openly criticized the Kremlin tend to suddenly become the subject of criminal investigation into their (admittedly often murky) business activities. Meanwhile others, with equally dubious reputations, remain untouched.

Financial markets

Financial markets more or less vanished overnight on 17 August 1998, and what remained came increasingly under the control of the CBR. The positive side of this was that companies and financial organizations stopped devoting all their energy to speculation. Companies are now reinvesting their profits, and an increase in bank lending to the real sector is slowly under way as banks are forced to turn to 'traditional bank activities' in search of profits. The absence of financial markets also means that Russia is no longer host to international 'hot money', which would quickly flee the country in case of a change in sentiment, turning a problem into a crisis as happened in 1998.

The political scene

Significant changes have also taken place in the political arena. Many radical reformers left the government in the period right after the crisis. Those who stayed began to speak a different language, talking about strengthening the state, increasing support to the military complex, and rebuilding ties with the former USSR, in particular with Belarus. However, these words did not turn into action. Generally, action was not high on the agenda in the immediate post-crisis period, which was dominated by political inertia and passiveness. This passivity meant that important measures, such as a programme to deal with the mess of Russia's banking sector, were not developed, but it also prevented the authorities from making disastrous mistakes. Avoiding more mistakes was important for top officials in the Kremlin, who had started to look for a suitable successor for the increasingly unpopular Boris Yeltsin.

Before the crisis, relationships between the president, government and the Duma were characterized by conflicts which prevented progress on important reform measures. This stalemate remained more or less in place until Yeltsin's resignation on 1 January 2000. The scene changed with the election of Vladimir Putin as president in 2000 and the birth of the new Putin-allied party, Unity, which won the largest number of seats in parliamentary elections. The anti-reform element in the Duma was marginalized, and executive and legislature started working together, creating a platform for approval of long-awaited reform legislation.

BACK TO THE FUTURE?

One area where progress since the crisis has been limited is development of the investment and business climate. Some of the authors in this book have presented their relevant experience, and set out what has been done and what needs to be done in order to bring Russia back into global capital markets.

Russia's troubled transition has been associated with major gains and losses for investors. So far, success or failure has depended partly on access to well-connected individuals or the ability to 'buy' those connections. This adds further risk to an already risky climate, as well as having negative consequences for the creation of competitive markets. It is clear that the economy can be successful in attracting investment only if economic actors, domestic or foreign, are operating on a level playing field with equal treatment, legal protection and clearly stated 'rules of the game'.

This book has presented different stories from some of the front-line market makers and analysts in Russia. There is a consensus that investing in Russia has been and still is a real adventure. With its knot of bureaucracy, corruption and lack of legal protection, Russia has even been dubbed the 'Wild East'. But it should not be forgotten that many other countries have also gone through a phase in their development that has been more or less 'wild'. The positive message of many contributions here is that Russia's new economic and political environment opens the way for changes that will tame the Wild East and allow the Russian economy to normalize. However, that is not to deny that there is still a long way to go before we can talk about Russia as a fully fledged, properly functioning market economy.

LOOKING AHEAD

A key asset for Russia's future is the new post-Soviet generation. A large part of Russia's scientific base has been destroyed by a decade of economic and political turmoil. The brain-drain is a serious problem, as Russians studying abroad often prefer not to return. Economic progress is vital for creating opportunities for the well-educated part of the population and reversing the brain-drain. In this respect, initiatives such as the Economics Education and Research Consortium (EERC), the New Economic School, the Tacis-funded Russian European Centre for Economic Policy (RECEP), and the recent establishment of Russia's first home-grown independent think-tank, the Centre for Economic and Financial Research (CEFIR) are aiming to create a new-generation scientific base, as well as helping to reverse the brain-drain.

> **Russia's passage to a market economy has proved unpredictable.**

Russia's passage to a market economy has proved unpredictable. After so many wrong forecasts, analysts and investors are reluctant to predict developments. One indicator not to be underestimated is the change in beliefs and sentiments of Russians themselves. In this respect there have been some encouraging developments which are worth emphasizing. The Consumer Sentiment Index, produced by the Russian Centre for Public Opinion Research, has now risen beyond its previous peak of 1997, although the real income of the population is lower than it was then. The main explanation is that, in contrast with 1997, workers are now being paid in cash and on time. This feel-good factor has led consumers to be more positive about Russia's (near) future. The same goes for Russian businesses. The Industrial Confidence Index, produced by the Institute for the Economy in Transition, is showing increased confidence of managers in the development of their companies.

There are also positive signs in the foreign investment statistics. Although absolute investment levels remain low, there is an observable increase in foreign investments originating from countries such as Cyprus and Luxembourg, widely believed to be the return of flight capital. Russian businessmen are beginning to trust their own country sufficiently to repatriate capital.

However, as sure as night follows day, foreign and exiled Russian capital will come to Russia in large quantities only if the investment climate and investment opportunities improve. This is the only way to reverse capital flight on a large scale, and draw the interest of foreign investors. In this respect there will be a major step forward in summer 2001 if the Duma approves law drafts on land ownership, further tax reform, red tape reduction and measures against money laundering. If they are adopted and (more critically) implemented, these measures will have a significant impact on the way business is done in Russia.

Notes

[1]Dutch Disease affected energy-producing countries such as Holland (hence the name), the UK and Norway during the oil crises of the 1970s. Large capital inflows due to high world oil prices led to real exchange rate appreciation, reducing the competitiveness of the manufacturing sector in these countries.

[2]This trend had started already under Gorbachev and *perestroika*.

INDEX